Marriage, Divorce, Remarriag

SOCIAL TRENDS IN THE UNITED STATES

Social Science Research Council
Center for Coordination of Research
on Social Indicators

Marriage
Divorce
Remarriage

ANDREW J. CHERLIN

HARVARD UNIVERSITY PRESS

Cambridge, Massachusetts
and London, England

• **Library of Congress Cataloging in Publication Data**

Cherlin, Andrew J., 1948–
  Marriage, divorce, remarriage.

  (Social trends in the United States)
  Includes bibliographical references and index.
    1. Marriage—United States. 2. Divorce—United
States. 3. Remarriage—United States. 4. Family—
United States. 5. Afro-American families. I. Title.
II. Series.
HQ535.C415   306.8'0973   81-2901
ISBN 0-674-55080-3 (cloth)   AACR2
ISBN 0-674-55081-1 (paper)

To Bea and Al

Foreword

Over fifty years ago, Herbert Hoover established the President's Research Committee on Social Trends to study social changes. The committee's report, *Recent Social Trends in the United States*, edited by William F. Ogburn and published in 1933, was a landmark in the study of social change and a model for communicating the results of academic research to the general public.

In the half century since that time, social scientists have collected data on a great variety of statistical time series which measure changes in American society. These data permit tracking, with high standards of reliability, the changing attitudes, behavior, and living conditions of the population. Concurrently we have developed concepts, such as cohort analysis, and statistical tools, such as methods for the simultaneous analysis of many variables, which greatly increase our ability to make inferences from data. Finally, we have produced a stock of findings, empirical generalizations, and theories of society and its changes which guide inquiry and the ordering of observations.

These developments have offered challenges as well as new resources to those who would describe and understand the changes taking place in American society. The accumulated data can be overwhelming, and findings that rely upon new analytic concepts and sophisticated statistical methods can be difficult to communicate even to colleagues.

Marriage, Divorce, Remarriage is the first volume in a series by leading social scientists who will write about continuities and changes in the society in a manner that can be understood by those without advanced technical training. The series, Social Trends in the United States, is designed to present to the general public recent scholarship on and current analyses of topics of broad interest and concern. We hope that our scientific colleagues will find these volumes accurate and responsible treatments of topics of scientific as well as public importance.

The series is a project of the Social Science Research Council's Center for Coordination of Research on Social Indicators. The center was established in 1972 with funding from the Division of Social and Economic Science of the National Science Foundation for the purpose of enhancing the contribution of the social sciences to the development of a broad range of indicators of social change in response to demands from the research and policy communities. Staffed by a small group of social scientists, the center operates under the intellectual guidance of the council's Advisory and Planning Committee on Social Indicators: Albert J. Reiss, Jr., Yale University, Chairman; Erik Allardt, University of Helsinki; Richard Berk, University of California; Richard H. Bolt, Massachusetts Institute of Technology (retired); Martin H. David, University of Wisconsin; James A. Davis, Harvard University; Gudmund Hernes, University of Bergen; Kenneth C. Land, University of Illinois; William M. Mason, University of Michigan; John Modell, University of Minnesota; Stephen H. Schneider, National Center for Atmospheric Research; and Nancy B. Tuma, Stanford University.

The concept of the series was developed under the leadership of Philip E. Converse when he was chairman of the committee from 1975 to 1978. The committee's interest in social reporting and its ideas about this series owe much to Otis Dudley Duncan, the first chairman, and to Eleanor Bernert Sheldon and former members of the committee: Richard A. Easterlin, Stephen E. Fienberg, Leo A. Goodman, Robert M. Hauser, Gary C. Koch, Stanley Lebergott, Mancur Olson, Arthur Stinchcombe, Leroy

O. Stone, Natalie Rogoff Ramsøy, Wolfgang Zapf, and Harriet
Zuckerman. Donald J. Hernandez was primarily responsible for staff work
on the present volume. Other members of the center staff who
have contributed to the development of the series include Nancy
McManus, David E. Myers, Robert Pearson, and Richard C.
Rockwell. Roberta Balstad Miller has provided overall coordination for the series.

Robert Parke

Director, Center for Coordination
  of Research on Social Indicators
Social Science Research Council

Acknowledgments

Throughout the planning and writing of this book, I worked closely with the staff of the Center for Coordination of Research on Social Indicators of the Social Science Research Council, particularly Robert Parke, the director, and Donald J. Hernandez. Without Bob Parke's enthusiasm for this project and Don Hernandez's willingness to assist me in any way he could, this book would not exist. I am grateful to them and to the center for its support.

A number of scholars reviewed all or part of the manuscript. These people gave generously of their time, providing me with detailed critiques to guide my revisions. The final product is, I believe, much improved because of their suggestions. I wish to thank Richard Easterlin, Glen Elder, Doris Entwisle, Reynolds Farley, Frank Furstenberg, Nathan Glazer, Mavis Hetherington, Robert Hill, John Modell, Arthur Norton, Valerie Oppenheimer, Ronald Rindfuss, Richard Rubinson, Wade Smith, James Sweet, Maris Vinovskis, Harold Watts, and Robert Weiss.

I am grateful to the following publishers for permission to use material from two articles I have published previously: "Remarriage as an Incomplete Institution," by permission of

The University of Chicago Press, copyright © 1978 by The University of Chicago; and "Cohabitation: How the French and Swedes Do It," from *Psychology Today*, copyright © 1979 Ziff Davis Publishing Company.

I also wish to thank Michael Aronson of Harvard University Press for his encouragement and assistance. In addition, I am grateful to Pamela Walters, who provided valuable research assistance throughout this project, and to Deborah Holtzman, who assisted ably with some of the calculations in chapter 1. Finally, I thank Joanne Hildebrandt for her excellent secretarial assistance.

A.C.

Contents

Marriage, Divorce, Remarriage

Introduction

Consider the following hypothetical life history. When Bill was ten, his parents separated. He lived with his mother and saw his father every Saturday. Four years later, his mother remarried, and Bill added a stepfather to his family. At eighteen, Bill left home to attend college, and after graduation he and his girlfriend moved in together. A year and a half later they married, and soon afterward they had a child. After several years, however, the marriage began to turn sour. Bill and his wife eventually separated, with Bill's wife retaining custody of the child. Three years later Bill married a woman who had a child from a previous marriage, and together they had another child. Bill's second marriage lasted thirty-five years, until his death.

By the time he entered middle age, Bill had lived in six family or familylike settings: first in his parents' household, then in a single-parent family headed by his mother, then in a family formed by his mother's remarriage, then in a cohabiting relationship with his girlfriend, then in his first marriage, and finally in his second marriage. He had accumulated a large number of kin and quasi-kin: his mother, father, stepfather, first wife, second wife, two children, and his stepchild, not to mention more distant kin such as grandparents, stepgrandparents, and two sets of in-laws. And at one time or another he had had dealings with people to whom he was related only by the ties of broken marriages, such as his father's second wife, his first wife's second husband, and his second wife's first husband.

Most young people today won't pass through all of the events in this example, but if the levels of marriage, divorce, remarriage, and cohabitation don't decrease in the near future, a substantial minority will. And many more will have family histories only slightly less complicated. In the 1950s someone with a family history this complex would have been rare; in the 1980s it is no longer unusual. The contrast between the 1980s and the 1950s might lead us to ask: why are the common patterns of marrying and divorcing so different from what they were just a few decades ago? And what are the consequences of these changes for the lives of adults and children and for our society as a whole?

Now is a good time to try to answer these questions, because the pace of change in marriage, divorce, and other aspects of family life appears to have abated for the moment. In the late 1940s and the 1950s young adults tended to marry earlier than they had at any time during the century, the birth rate rose to a twentieth-century high, and the divorce rate remained unusually steady. But in the 1960s and 1970s the average age at marriage rose, the birth rate dropped to an all-time low, and the divorce rate more than doubled. As we enter the 1980s, all of these rates are changing more slowly, and some of the trends may be shifting direction again. Since the mid-1970s, for example, the marriage and birth rates have increased by small amounts and the divorce rate has not been rising as fast. We may have at least a short interval of less rapid change in marriage and family life—a period in which we can pause to take stock of the changes that have occurred in recent decades in marriage and divorce, to investigate the causes of these changes, and to examine their likely consequences.

During the early 1970s, as wave after wave of statistics about the changes in family life washed into our consciousness through news reports and scholarly accounts, a number of commentators predicted that the family as we know it would not survive much longer. Yet these forebodings are nothing new— for at least a century American observers have warned of the consequences of rising divorce, falling birth rates, and other changes in family life. "The family, in its old sense," wrote a contributor to the *Boston Quarterly Review* of October 1859, "is disappearing from our land, and not only our free institutions are threatened but the very existence of our society is endangered."[1] Whenever the pace of change quickens—particularly when the divorce rate is increasing rapidly—these sentiments reappear. When the concern about divorce grew in the 1970s, however, some scholars countered with evidence that the changes had been exaggerated and that in any case the family was a flexible institution that was unlikely to fade away.[2] By the end of the 1970s, when the pace of change had slowed again, the more sanguine view prevailed. Even social critic Christopher Lasch, whose writings had contributed to the concern, stated in a recent review that the dispute over whether the family had a future was a "false and meaningless issue."[3]

Nevertheless, all the commentators agree that the postwar changes in family patterns have significantly altered the lives of many Americans. Although the family undoubtedly has a future, its present form differs from its past form in important respects, at least in part because of the recent changes in patterns of marrying, divorcing, and remarrying. A smaller proportion of families today than in the 1950s resemble the two-biological-parents-with-children family which has been the norm in the United States. Instead, a greater proportion consist of single parents and their children or families formed by remarriage after divorce. Because of the sharp rise in divorce, the common assumption that a family occupies one household is increasingly incorrect. Although separation and divorce break the bonds between father and mother, the bonds between children and parents tend to remain intact. Consequently, an increasing number of families extend across two or three or more households, linked by the continuing ties between parents and children who live apart. Under these circumstances kinship ties are more complex and far-reaching than in families formed by first marriages. And even the definition of a family can become problematic—a child whose mother and father have divorced and remarried may define the members of his family differently from either of his parents.

The roller-coaster pattern of rapid change in marriage and divorce may, itself, have strained the capacity of the family to adapt, much as rapid change would strain the adaptive capacity of any social institution. The rapid pace also may have strained our cognitive capacity to make sense out of what has been going on. Just as we arrived at an understanding of the changes in family life, the trends shifted again. It may be useful, consequently, to look back over family change during the entire postwar period from the vantage point of the—at least temporarily —more stable early 1980s.

Family change is a broad topic, and any coherent report must be selective in its coverage. Because my focus is on the formation and dissolution of marriage and its causes and consequences, I do not have much to say about many other significant trends in husband-wife or parent-child relationships. For example, during the postwar period the proportion of two-parent families in which both husband and wife were employed increased sharply. These families faced new and challenging problems in integrating their work lives with satisfying family lives. Regrettably, a detailed discussion of these problems and of other topics not directly related to the theme of this book would take us too far afield.

Nor is this a report on trends in childbearing, an important topic that is complex enough to deserve a report of its own. Yet obviously there are close connections between trends in marriage and divorce, on the one hand, and trends in childbearing, so I do examine some aspects of these trends to increase our understanding of changes in marital formation and dissolution.

Because this is a study of overall trends in American society in the last several decades, it does not include much discussion of the differences among ethnic, religious, and regional groups. There is evidence that many intergroup differences have declined in the postwar period. For instance, as I note below, Catholics appear to have become more similar to Protestants in their childbearing patterns and in their propensity to divorce. In addition, we lack adequate data on many group differences. The statements I make in chapters 1, 2, and 3, then, apply to Americans in general, although I try to alert the reader when there are sharp deviations among particular groups. Yet strong racial differences exist in many aspects of family life, including marriage and divorce, and some of these differences have become more pronounced during the postwar period. For this reason, in chapter 4 I discuss the differences between the typical patterns of marriage among blacks and whites.

My focus also means that I do not examine many of the so-called alternative lifestyles to marriage: communal living, gay couples, lifelong singlehood, and so forth. Although these ways of living are interesting in their own right, on a societal level the number of people involved in them is small compared to the number of ever-married persons. I do, however, discuss the phenomenal increase in the 1970s in cohabitation, a new stage of intimacy for young adults prior to marriage. And I examine the growth of single-parent families—much of which can be traced to the increase in separation and divorce—and the consequences of living in these families as a lone parent or as a child.

My first task is to take a long, hard look at the demographic data on trends in marriage, divorce, and remarriage, as well as the trends in such closely allied topics as cohabitation, single-parent families, and childbearing. Only by determining rigorously what did and did not happen to families in the postwar period is it possible to amass the factual base needed to probe the causes and consequences of the trends. The indicators I examine in chapter 1 should help us decide where to look for explanations of the trends and point to the important consequences. Moreover, a careful look at the record should disabuse us of any misleading common notions about the trends. For example, there is evidence to contradict the conventional wisdom that the family patterns of the 1970s were more unusual, in a historical sense, than the family patterns of the 1950s. Chapter 2 examines promising explanations, and chapter 3 explores the consequences of the trends for husbands and wives and for parents and children. Chapter 4 looks at the most prominent set of group differences in family patterns, the differences between the typical experiences of black and white Americans.

1
The Trends

We often think of social change in terms of the differences between one generation and the next—between our parents' lives and our own lives or between our own lives and our children's lives. When we look at the trends in marriage, divorce, and remarriage in the United States since World War II, the experiences of two successive generations stand in sharp contrast: the men and women who married and had children in the late 1940s and 1950s, and their sons and daughters, who entered adulthood in the late 1960s and 1970s. Most of the members of the older generation were born in the 1920s and the 1930s, and they grew up during the Great Depression and the war years. This group is relatively small because fewer babies were born during the late 1920s and the hard times of the 1930s. But when they reached adulthood, this generation had a large number of children. About five out of six of the women whose peak childbearing years occurred in the 1950s gave birth to at least two children, and those births were bunched at an earlier time in their lives.[1] The result was a great increase in births between the end of World War II and 1960, an increase which we now call the postwar baby boom. In 1957, at the peak of the boom, 4.3 million babies were born in the United States, compared to 2.4 million in 1937. (By comparison, there were 3.5 million births in 1979.) Thus the relatively small generation of parents in the 1950s gave birth to a much larger generation—the children of the baby boom.[2]

In the 1950s, when the members of the older generation were in their twenties and thirties, the country's marriage rate was high and rising, and its divorce rate was relatively low and stable. But as the younger generation matured, all that changed. The divorce rate began to rise in the early 1960s and doubled between 1966 and 1976. As more and more young people put off marrying, the marriage rate fell, though the number of couples living together without marrying more than doubled in the 1970s. The birth rate fell to an all-time low.

In this chapter I compare the experiences of these two generations as they have married, divorced, and remarried. But we must be careful not to assume that just because the older generation came first, their family patterns were more typical of twentieth-century American family life. Put another way, we shouldn't assume that all the changes since the 1950s were deviations from the usual way of family life in the United States. In fact, I argue that the 1950s were the more unusual time, that the timing of marriage in the 1970s was closer to the typical twentieth-century pattern than was the case in the 1950s. The divorce experiences of both generations differed from the long-term trend in divorce. In addition, the rate of childbearing in the 1950s was unusually high by twentieth-century standards. A close look at the historical record, then, suggests that in some ways the 1970s were more consistent with long-term trends in family life than were the 1950s.

In order to back up statements such as these, the mass of statistical information on family life must be shaped into a coherent picture of the lifetime experiences of men and women. And that requires a clear definition of two key terms: "cohort" and "generation." By a cohort, I mean a group of people who were born during the same time period. The period can be one year or several years, depending on the kinds of topics being investigated. By a generation, I mean a group of people who are the ascendent or descendent kin of another group: grandparents, parents, children, grandchildren, and the like.

A generation usually comprises several successive cohorts; just how many depends on how narrowly we define the time period for each cohort. Take, for example, the men and women who had children during the late 1940s and the 1950s. It is sometimes useful to think of these people as a generation because they are the parents of the children of the baby boom. Most of these parents were born in the 1920s and 1930s, although a small minority were born earlier and a handful were born later. We could conceivably consider everyone born between 1920 and 1939 as members of one cohort. Yet the experiences of a person born in 1920 (who was nine when the depression struck) were probably quite different from the experiences of someone born in 1936 (who was nine when World War II ended). In studying the parental generation of the 1950s, then, it may be more enlightening to separate them into at least two cohorts—those born in the 1920s and those born in the 1930s—and investigate the differing lifetime experiences of each cohort.

Demographers use the term "cohort analysis" to refer to the strategy of dividing a generation into its constituent cohorts and tracing the lifetime experiences of each. If used properly, this method can provide new insights into social trends, and I rely on it often in the pages that follow.

ENTERING MARRIAGE

One hardly needs to have the latest national statistics to know that young adults are not marrying as quickly as they were just ten or twenty years ago. Anyone who knows recent college graduates, for example, realizes that more and more of them are postponing marriage until their mid- or late twenties. Getting married within weeks of graduation—seemingly a symbol of success for many college women in the 1950s and early 1960's —is now much less common. In the past decade there also has been a great increase in the number of young adults who have moved in with someone of the opposite sex without marrying first. Some observers have expressed concern that the later age at marriage and the increase in "cohabitation" or "living together" might indicate a weakening of our system of marriage and family life. Others are more sanguine but believe that these changing patterns of coupling will alter American family life.

Almost every adult in the United States eventually marries, although in some eras people tend to marry earlier than in others. In the postwar period there have been sharp fluctuations in the timing of marriage, with an especially noticeable difference between the 1950s and the 1970s, as can be seen by comparing the lifetime experiences of several cohorts. Figure 1-1 shows the actual and projected marriage experiences of women born in the periods 1910 to 1914, 1920 to 1924, 1930 to 1934, 1940 to 1944, and 1950 to 1954. The graph displays for

Figure 1-1 Cumulative percentage of all marriages occurring by a given age, for five birth cohorts of women from 1910 to 1954. (For sources, see Appendix 1.)

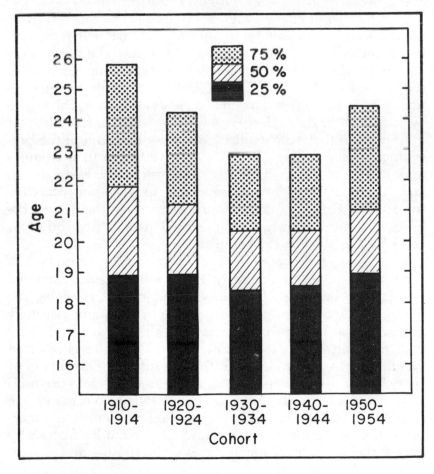

each cohort the estimated age at which 25, 50, and 75 percent of those who will ever marry have already done so.[3]

Figure 1-1 shows that there has been little change in the age by which one-quarter of all those women who will ever marry have done so. The age at which 50 percent have married—the median age of marrying for each cohort—shows more change. It was highest for the oldest cohort, then it declined by about one and one-half years for women born in the 1930s and 1940s, and more recently it has risen again. The figure that shows the most change is the age at which three-fourths have married: it was above twenty-five years for the 1910–1914 cohort, fell below twenty-three for the middle cohorts, and now has risen above twenty-four for the youngest cohort.

This pattern of change suggests that so far in this century a fixed proportion of women in any cohort marry early, regardless of the historical circumstances. Conversely, the variation in the timing of marriage mainly reflects the changing behavior of those women who tend to wait until their early twenties to marry. Among women born in the 1930s and 1940s, those who remained single through their teenage years married relatively quickly when they reached their early twenties. But in the preceding and succeeding cohorts, single women in their twenties took longer to marry. As a result, the spread between the 25 and 75 percent marks decreased from nearly seven years for the 1910 to 1914 cohort to about four years in the middle cohorts, and more recently it has increased to about five and a half years for the 1950 to 1954 cohort.

These changes do not necessarily imply that large numbers of the young women of the early 1980s will remain unmarried throughout their lives. Currently, as Figure 1-1 suggests, the timing of marriage for young women is becoming increasingly similar to that of cohorts born early in the century, and more than nine out of ten women in these older cohorts married eventually.[4] In fact, more than 90 percent of the members of every birth cohort on record (records extend back to the mid-1800s) have eventually married.[5] The adults who came of age after World War II have the highest lifetime percentage married—96.4 percent for females and 94.1 percent for males who were at their most marriageable ages in the 1950s—and it is unlikely that the children of the baby boom will reach this level.[6] But the higher proportion of single young adults in the 1970s and early 1980s suggests only that they are marrying later, not foregoing marriage. It is unlikely that their lifetime proportions marrying will fall below the historical minimum of 90 percent.

Figure 1-1 demonstrates that the women in the middle cohorts tended to marry sooner than women born early in the century as well as women born at mid-century. This difference suggests that the timing of marriage among women born during the depression and the war years may have been less typical of twentieth-century patterns than the marital timing of women born during the baby boom. We can obtain additional evidence by studying the long-term trend in the proportion of all men and women aged twenty to twenty-four in a given year who have never married. As we saw above, women in this age range appear to have provided much of the variation in the timing of marriage. Figure 1-2 graphs the percentage of women and men twenty to twenty-four years old who had never married from 1890—the earliest year for which we have information—to 1979. We can see from this graph that the percentages changed very little between 1890 and 1940. But after 1940, when those

Figure 1-2 Percentage never married for men and women aged 20 to 24, 1890 to 1979. (Sources: for 1890–1970, U.S. Bureau of the Census, *Historical Statistics of the United States, Colonial Times to 1970*, pp. 20–21; for 1979, Current Population Reports, series P-20, no. 349, "Marital Status and Living Arrangements," Table 1.)

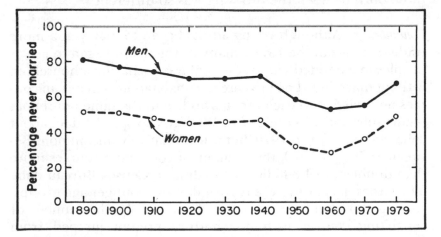

who were born in the 1920s entered adulthood, the percentage never married decreased sharply. It stayed low during the years when people born during the depression and the war reached their early twenties. More recently, as the men and women born during the baby boom have reached their early twenties, the percentage never married has returned to its earlier, higher levels.

This trend is especially pronounced for women; by 1979 the percentage never married of women aged twenty to twenty-four had risen to pre-1940 levels. For men the percentage never married also rose after the 1950s, but it remained somewhat below prewar levels. Consequently, although some commentators have argued that the trend toward later marriage in the 1970s represents a deviation from traditional patterns of family formation, the historical record suggests otherwise. The timing of marriage among the baby boom cohorts—whose members tended to marry in the 1970s and early 1980s—is in line with the pattern observed in the 1890 to 1940 period; it is the cohorts born between the early 1920s and World War II whose behavior is problematic. It is justifiable to say that in the 1970s marriage was being "postponed" only if the unusual decade of the 1950s is chosen as the frame of reference. (This does not imply, however, that the reasons why today's young adults are marrying later are the same as those of persons born at the turn of the century.) In chapter 2 I discuss why the marital timing of those born between the two wars was so different.[7]

Cohabitation. Although young adults began to marry at a more traditional age in the 1970s, many of them also began to live as couples in a decidedly untraditional way—sharing a household without marrying. The increase in cohabitation—that is, in couples not married to each other who live in the same household —was substantial in the 1970s. We have no specific data about cohabitation prior to 1970, but it was relatively uncommon. Between 1970 and 1979, the number of cohabiting couples more than doubled, to 1,346,000, according to Census Bureau data. The largest increases were reported in the younger age groups. Among those under twenty-five, for example, the number of cohabiting couples with no children present jumped from

29,000 in 1970 to 274,000 in 1979—an eightfold increase. Between 1977 and 1979 alone, the number of cohabiting couples identified by the Census Bureau's Current Population Survey increased by 40 percent.[8]

Some of the increase was caused by the increasing numbers of young adults in the population, as the baby boom cohorts moved through young adulthood. But the increase in cohabitation was far too large to be accounted for solely by this shift in the age structure of the population. Another part of the increase may have been spurious—the result of the lessening reluctance of cohabiting couples to disclose their living arrangements to an interviewer. The Bureau of the Census arrived at its estimates of cohabitation by counting all persons living in households containing two (and only two) unrelated adults of the opposite sex. Most of these persons undoubtedly were involved in an intimate relationship with their housemates, but an unknown proportion may have been sharing an apartment and nothing more. Other than census data, there is little information about the extent of cohabitation in the United States. Despite these limitations, however, most of the increase seems real, especially to anyone who has observed the living arrangements of young adults during the decade. Even if the increase was not as spectacular as the census figures suggest, it was still impressive.

We don't know what proportion of the young adults of the 1970s have cohabited. Of the twenty- to thirty-year-old men in a 1975 national study, 18 percent replied that they had lived as a partner for six months or more with a woman to whom they were not married at the time; two-thirds of these cohabitants had done so only once.[9] But some of those surveyed will cohabit at some point in their lives, so that the 18 percent figure underestimates the lifetime proportion of young men who will cohabit. Moreover, the rise in cohabitation in the latter half of the 1970s suggests that 1975 figures may now be out of date.

The scant information we have suggests that living together has become more common among two different groups of urban young adults: a better-educated group who tend to cohabit prior to marrying, and a less-well-educated group whose relationships are more likely to include at least one previously married partner.[10] The better-educated cohabitants fit the popular image—never-married, unconventional, college-educated couples. But a 1978 Bureau of the Census survey showed that not all cohabiting couples fit this image: 35 percent of all cohabiting adults under age thirty-five have been previously married, and some of them were still married but living with someone else.[11] Although we cannot yet say for sure, it looks as if cohabitation may have become a living arrangement common to two very different groups at opposite ends of the social spectrum.

Implications. How might these changes—the increase in cohabitation and the later age at marriage—affect patterns of family life in the United States? As for cohabitation, it may be too soon to assess its significance, but we can draw some tentative conclusions. When the rise in cohabitation first attracted attention in the early 1970s, some researchers believed it to be a radical departure from traditional patterns of family formation. "The living together relationship," wrote two scholars in 1973, "may come to represent a universal substitute for marriage for adults of all ages."[12] But casual observation and further research soon suggested otherwise. A 1975 national survey of men aged twenty to thirty showed that among those who had cohabited once and married once, 37 percent married the persons with whom they had cohabited.[13] Without doubt, other men in the survey had cohabited more than once and then married one of their partners, while still others were likely to have cohabited and then married after 1975. Another study of 1,200 college students from fourteen state universities reported that nearly all of the students who had cohabited wished to marry at some time in the future.[14] Other studies suggest that cohabiting couples tend to live together for a relatively short time before either breaking up or marrying. For instance, the 1975 survey of young men showed that the proportion who were living with someone at the time of the survery (5 percent) was much less than the proportion who had ever cohabited for six months or more (18 percent), a discrepancy which implies that the relationships were of short duration.[15] The evidence is still indirect and tentative, but it suggests that for most young adults, cohabitation is not a lifelong alternative to marriage but rather a stage of intimacy that precedes (or sometimes follows) marriage.

Young adults appear to be cohabiting as a way of finding a compatible partner, whom they often marry. It may be, then, that the increase in cohabitation will have little effect on the lifetime chances that a young adult will ever marry.

Still, most studies of cohabitation in the United States have been limited to college students, and we have only the barest national statistics on its prevalence. In Western Europe, where cohabitation also increased sharply in the 1970s, more detailed information is available. Recent studies in Sweden and France, in particular, reveal two different patterns of cohabitation. In the absence of adequate information from the United States, it is worth examining the Swedish and French data to see whether they can help us interpret our own situation.

According to Jan Trost of the University of Uppsala, 99 percent of all young Swedish couples today live together before they marry. The country's marriage rate dropped sharply in the 1970s, and in 1976 one out of three children was born out of wedlock (compared with one out of seven in the United States). Out of every one hundred couples in Sweden in 1978, fifteen were unmarried (compared with two out of one hundred in the United States). In Sweden, then, cohabitation appears to be a nearly universal stage in an intimate relationship, and an increasing number of couples appear to be postponing marriage indefinitely or foregoing it altogether.[16]

In France, on the other hand, living together is common but far from universal. According to the results of a 1977 national survey conducted by Louis Roussel of the Institut National d'Études Démographiques, only 31 percent of married eighteen- to twenty-nine-year-olds said they had lived with their partners before marriage. The percentages were higher for young people who had a college education (54 percent), who lived in cities of over 200,000 (41 percent), or who came from middle-class backgrounds (45 percent). But living together was not just a middle-class phenomenon: 25 percent of those who had not attended college had cohabited before they married. A third of the couples who had cohabited said they had decided to marry before they began to live together, and another third said they had at least discussed the possibility of marriage. Few had children or planned to have children without marrying.[17]

Does either of these countries provide a guide to what might be happening in the United States? Americans tend to watch Sweden for hints about the future, as if any new social trend in Scandinavia automatically hits California a few years later and then seeps slowly eastward. But the Scandinavian countries have a long tradition of cohabitation; in past centuries, rural couples often lived together before marriage, and many children were born out of wedlock.[18] Rural Swedes often felt that the decision to marry was a private matter; Americans have always believed that marriage should be publicly approved by church and state. This difference, I think, makes it unlikely that cohabitation and out-of-wedlock births ever will be as widespread here as in Sweden.

The French situation seems closer to what Americans may be experiencing. Although there are no directly comparable figures for France and the United States, the French figure of 31 percent of married couples ever-cohabiting probably is not much higher than the true figure for this country. Eleanor D. Macklin reported that the various studies of college students in the United States suggest that about 25 percent have ever cohabited;[19] more will do so after they leave college.

If the French experience is an appropriate guide, it suggests that cohabitation is becoming a generally accepted, or at least tolerated, stage of life. Only 8 percent of the parents of cohabiting couples in the French survey were openly hostile to the arrangement, and about three-fourths of the couples reported that difficulties with landlords, employers, government forms, and so forth were rare or nonexistent. But this acceptance does not extend to couples who remain unmarried and have children; the majority of cohabiting young adults in France thought that couples who want children should marry first. Cohabitation appears to be a temporary stage in France: most young couples tended to cohabit for a year or two and then either break up or marry.

The small amount of information we have on cohabitation in the United States is, I believe, consistent with the French pattern. As I mentioned above, there is some evidence that young American adults, like their French counterparts, cohabit for a short period of time before either breaking up or marrying. Although we have no firm evidence about the acceptance of cohabitation in the United States, informal observation suggests that people's attitudes have become much more tolerant in the last decade. One sign of acceptance is the attempt to regulate the behavior of the cohabiting partners; in the past few years courts have begun to define partners' rights and obligations to each other.[20] The legal rulings, the short duration of many cohabiting relationships, the public's increasing tolerance, the indications that many cohabiting couples eventually marry—all these pieces of evidence point to the conclusion that in the United States, as in France, cohabitation is being institutionalized as part of the family system. Far from being a threat to the primacy of marriage in American family patterns, cohabitation is becoming more and more like the first stage of marriage.

Some writers argue that cohabitation will enhance personal growth, lead to a better choice of marriage partners, and lower the divorce rate.[21] To be sure, cohabitation is a trial relationship of sorts, a way for men and women to develop and test feelings of intimacy and to assess their mutual compatibility. It is reasonable to expect that some incompatible couples who might have married and then divorced had they been born a decade or two earlier will now cohabit and then separate without ever marrying. These *de facto* divorces will never show up in the divorce rate. To the extent, then, that cohabitation allows adults to refine their criteria for choosing spouses and to dissolve unsuccessful relationships, it should lower the amount of divorce.

Yet I suspect that the overall effect of cohabitation on the probability of divorce may well be negligible or even work in the opposite direction. It seems to me that cohabitation carries with it the ethic that a relationship should be ended if either partner is dissatisfied; this, after all, is part of the reason why people live together rather than marrying. Most people who choose to cohabit either subscribe to this ethic beforehand or soon learn to do so. I would argue that they are likely to carry over this individualistic ethic to their marriages. On the other hand, unmarried adults who do not cohabit may have a more traditional view of the sanctity of the marriage bond, and they may bring this traditional attitude to their marriages. If so, then the probability of divorce for married couples who first cohabited might be the same or even higher than the probability for those who didn't cohabit. And the rise in cohabitation might have little effect on the national rate of divorce.

As for the returning trend to marrying at an older age, it doesn't appear that this will have a major impact on lifetime levels of marriage or on the rate of divorce. It seems likely that nine out of ten of today's young adults will eventually marry, although at a later age, on average, than in the 1950s. With respect to divorce, we know that people who marry at an older age have had a lower probability of separation and divorce.[22] One might argue that the trend toward later marriage should help people pick more suitable partners and therefore that it should help hold down the divorce rate. The trouble with this argument is that the average age at marriage was rising throughout the 1960s and 1970s, but during that time the divorce rate doubled. Those who believe in the influence of age at marriage on society-wide levels of divorce are left with the weak counterargument that the divorce rate might have risen even faster had the average age at marriage not increased. Although later age at marriage is associated with lower probability of divorce for individuals, later age at marriage appears to have only a slight influence on the overall level of divorce.

The trend toward later marriage probably has contributed to the recent decline in childbearing, because women who marry later tend to bear fewer children. Most women do not give birth until they marry, and the older a woman is when she marries, the fewer years remain in which she is biologically able to have children. In addition, the later a woman marries, the older she is when she has borne all the children she wants, and the fewer years remain in which she is exposed to the risks of unintended pregnancy.[23] When the average age at marriage is rising, many women are in effect postponing childbearing for a few years, which reduces the current number of births. Thus the later age at marriage influences the timing of childbearing. I suspect, however, that any further rise in the average age at marriage, unless quite drastic, would be unlikely to lower the lifetime levels of childbearing much further. Women who marry in their mid- or even late twenties have plenty of reproductive years in which to have two births—the current level of lifetime fertility. An older age at marriage, moreover, does allow many women to be employed longer or to receive more education before they marry. This change, I suspect, is significant for some young women, giving them a greater opportunity to develop market-able skills and establish themselves in the labor force before they marry. Because of this greater investment they may be less likely to drop out of the labor force after they marry, and this in turn may tend to depress the rate of childbearing. Or it could help ensure that more women will return to the labor force after a possible interruption for childbearing.

On balance, neither the increase in cohabitation nor the later age at marriage portends major changes in patterns of mar-riage, divorce, and remarriage. Granted, the increase in cohabi-tation and the later age at marriage have altered the life course of young adults; in the space of a decade cohabitation has added an unprecedented new stage of intimacy. But as best we can tell, this new stage of intimacy tends to lead rapidly to the rejection of unsatisfactory partners and to the eventual choice of one partner as worthy of a long-term, public commitment. Most Americans continue to make this commitment in the form of marriage, although they may take a few years longer to do so than did the generation reaching adulthood in the 1950s.

CHILDBEARING

A brief look at trends in childbearing may tell us something about the differences between the parental generation of the 1950s and their children's generation. Most people are familiar with the broad outlines of the postwar trend in childbearing, or fertility, to use the demographer's term for childbearing: the annual birth rate spurted upward just after the war and then, after a brief respite, increased sharply during the 1950s. It then fell just as sharply in the 1960s and 1970s. We now know that during the 1950s women were having their first child earlier in their lives, and subsequent children were born closer together; after 1960 women had their first child at a later age and spaced subsequent children further apart.[24] These trends in the timing of fertility—the accelerated pace of the 1950s and the post-ponement of the 1960s and 1970s—amplified the peaks and valleys of the baby boom and bust as measured by annual birth rates. We can obtain a more meaningful picture of the trends by examining the lifetime levels of fertility for different cohorts. The lifetime levels measure changes in the volume of childbearing over time, independent of changes in the timing of births during women's reproductive years.

Figure 1-3 displays the cohort total fertility rate for single-year birth cohorts of women born between 1891 and 1950, based on data assembled by Norman B. Ryder. The cohort total fertility rate is the mean number of children born per woman in a particular cohort. For cohorts of women past their reproductive years, this rate can be calculated from survey or birth registration data; for the more recent cohorts, future levels of fertility must be estimated.[25] As can be seen in Figure 1-3, the mean

Figure 1-3 Cohort total fertility rate for single-year birth cohorts, 1891 to 1950. (Source: Norman B. Ryder, "Components of Temporal Variations in American Fertility," in Robert W. Hiorns, ed., *Demographic Patterns in Developed Societies* [London: Taylor and Francis, 1980], pp. 15–54.)

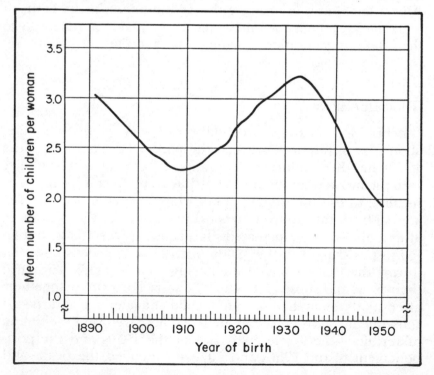

number of births per woman born in 1891 was 3.0. This figure, as best we can tell, declined throughout the nineteenth century: it was 4.1 for the 1867 cohort and perhaps 7 or 8 for those born in the early 1800s.[26] The total fertility rate declined to a low of 2.3 for the 1908 cohort—who came of age early in the depression—and then rose precipitously to a high of 3.2 for the 1933 cohort—who came of age in the 1950s—before beginning a steep slide to the estimated level of 1.9 for the 1950 cohort.

The graph demonstrates that trends in lifetime levels of childbearing in this century have followed a single, massive wave pattern that peaked with the cohorts of women who married and began to bear children in the decade following World War II. This great rise in fertility is at variance with the long-term historical decline in childbearing over the past 150 years. To be sure, Figure 1-3 and our sketchy knowledge of nineteenth-century fertility patterns also suggest that the fertility of the cohorts who reached adulthood during the depression was unusually low. And the fertility of the most recent cohorts appears to be at an all-time low, although that seems to be in line with the longer historical decline. The more unusual phenomenon, in a long-term perspective, is the great increase in childbearing among those born during the 1920s and 1930s. Cohort trends in childbearing, like trends in age at marriage, suggest that the cohorts who grew up during the depression and the war years—not the cohorts who grew up during the postwar years—stand out as more historically distinctive.

MARITAL DISSOLUTION

No trend in American family life since World War II has received more attention or caused more concern than the rising rate of divorce. The divorce rate, however, has been rising since at least the middle of the nineteenth century. Figure 1-4 shows the number of divorces per 1,000 existing marriages (after 1920, per 1,000 married women) in every year between 1860 (the earliest year for which data are available) and 1978. These are annual measures, reflecting the particular social and eco-

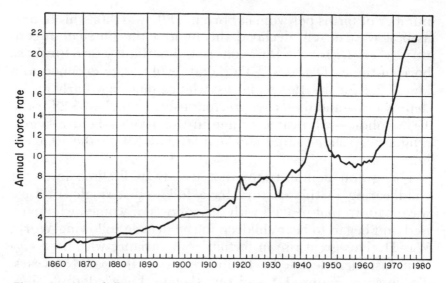

Figure 1-4 Annual divorce rates, United States. For 1920–1978: divorces per 1,000 married women aged 15 and over; for 1860–1920: divorces per 1,000 existing marriages. (Sources: 1860–1920, Paul H. Jacobson, *American Marriage and Divorce* [New York: Rinehart, 1959], Table 42; 1920–1967, U.S. National Center for Health Statistics, Vital and Health Statistics, series 21, no. 24, *100 Years of Marriage and Divorce Statistics* [1973], Table 4; 1968–1978, U.S. National Center for Health Statistics, Vital Statistics Report, Advance Report, vol. 29, no. 4, supplement, *Final Divorce Statistics 1978*, Table 2.)

nomic conditions of each year. We can see, for example, that the annual rate of divorce increased temporarily after every major war: there is a slight bulge in the graph following the Civil War, a rise in 1919 and 1920 following World War I, and a large spike in the years immediately after World War II. We can also see how the depression temporarily lowered the divorce rate in the early 1930s: with jobs and housing scarce, many couples had to postpone divorcing until they could afford to do so.

Ignoring for the moment the temporary movements induced by war and depression, there is a slow, steady increase in the annual rate of divorce through the end of World War II. Since the war, however, the graph looks somewhat different. In the period from 1950 to about 1962 the annual rates are lower than what we would expect on the basis of the long-term rise. Then starting about 1962, the annual rates rise sharply, so that by the end of the 1970s the rate of divorce is well above what would be predicted from the long-term trend. Thus if we compare the annual rates from the 1950s with those from the 1970s, as many observers have tended to do, we are comparing a period of relatively low rates with a time of very high rates. The result is to make the recent rise loom larger than it would if we took the long-term view.

It is true that the rise in annual divorce rates in the 1960s and 1970s is much steeper and more sustained than any increase in the past century, but to gauge the significance of this recent rise, it is necessary to consider the lifetime divorce experiences of adults, rather than just the annual rates of divorce. In Figure 1-5 the dotted line is an estimate of the proportion of all marriages begun in every year between 1867 and 1973 which have ended, or will end, in divorce before one of the spouses dies. Following conventional usage among demographers, I refer to all people marrying in a given year as a "marriage cohort." For marriage cohorts after 1910, the lifetime record is incomplete, and I have relied on projections prepared by Samuel H. Pres-

Figure 1-5 Proportion of marriages begun in each year that will end in divorce, 1867 to 1973. (Sources: see Appendix 2.)

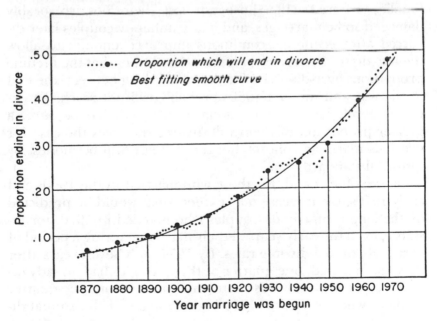

ton, John McDonald, and James Weed.[27] Any projection, of course, can be undermined by future events, so the importance of Figure 1-5 lies more in the general trends it shows than in its precise estimates for recent marriage cohorts. We can see from the dotted line that the proportion of all marriages in a given year that eventually end in divorce has increased at a faster and faster rate since the mid-nineteenth century. Moreover, the increase has been relatively steady, without the large fluctuations which the annual rates show in times of war or depression.

In order to make the underlying long-term trend clearer, the graph also shows the smooth curve that most closely fits the pattern of change in the proportions.[28] People who married in the years when the dotted line is above the smooth curve were more likely to become divorced than the long-term historical trend would lead us to expect; people who married in years when the dotted line is below the smooth curve were less likely to become divorced than would be expected. We can see, for instance, that although the annual divorce rates were temporarily low in the early 1930s, more of the people who married just before or during the depression eventually became divorced than we would expect from the long-term trend. The hardship and distress families suffered when husbands lost their jobs irrevocably damaged some marriages, and many unhappy couples later divorced after economic conditions improved enough to allow them to do so. Conversely, Figure 1-5 indicates that the lifetime proportions ever-divorced for those marrying between the end of the war and the late 1950s probably will not reach the expected levels based on the long-term trend. To be sure, a greater proportion of them will divorce than was the case for previous marriage cohorts, but the increase will be modest by historical standards.

On the other hand, for those who married in the 1960s and early 1970s, the increase may exceed what would be predicted by the long-term trend. Couples who married in 1970, for instance, lived the early years of their marriage during a period of very high annual divorce rates. By 1977, only seven years after they had married, one-quarter of these couples had already divorced. In contrast, it was twenty-five years before one-quarter of those who married in 1950 had divorced. If the annual divorce rates stay the same in the 1980s and 1990s as they were in 1977, 48 percent of those who married in 1970 will eventually divorce, according to a recent estimate.[29] As I discuss in later chapters, scholars disagree on how fast the divorce rate will increase in the near future, but almost no one expects a drop in the annual rates. Barring an unforeseen downturn in divorce in the near future, then, for those marrying in the late 1960s and early 1970s the lifetime proportions ever divorced are likely to be exceptionally high, even compared to the long-term rise in divorce.

In sum, although annual measures of divorce often show large fluctuations from year to year or decade to decade, the lifetime proportions ever divorced for people marrying in a given year have risen in a regular fashion for the past century, with some variations. Those who married during the depression and those who married in the 1960s and early 1970s experienced even higher levels of divorce over their lifetimes than the historical trend would predict. And those who married in the decade or so following the war were the only cohorts in the last hundred years to show a substantial, sustained shortfall in their lifetime levels of divorce. This latter group, of course, includes most of the parents of the baby boom children. Figure 1-5 suggests that the lifetime level of divorce for the baby boom parents was unusually low; for their children it will be unusually high.

Mortality. The other way in which a marriage can terminate, of course, is with the death of one spouse. Because mortality rates have declined in the twentieth century, the annual rate of death for married persons has declined at the same time that the annual rate of divorce has been rising. Some scholars have noted that as a result the total rate of marital dissolution—the number of marriages ending in either divorce or death in a given year per 1,000 existing marriages—hardly changed between 1860 and 1970. From 1860 to 1864 the combined rate was 33.2 dissolutions per 1,000 marriages; in 1970 the combined rate was 34.5.[30] Since 1970, however, the rising rate of divorce has pushed the total dissolution rate to an estimated 40.5 in 1978.[31] In the mid-nineteenth century, most of the dissolutions in a given year were caused by the death of one spouse, but by the mid-1970s, for the first time in our nation's history, more marriages ended every year in divorce than in death.[32] As long as the divorce rate continues to rise faster than the death rate for married persons falls, the total dissolution rate will continue to rise above the level of the past century.

Divorces tend to occur at a different stage of family life than deaths, and the two types of dissolution have different consequences for the remaining family members. Most people who divorce do so early in their marriage—about half of all divorces occur by the seventh year of marriage[33]—so that many divorces happen when children are still in the home. In the past, it was common for parents to die while their children were still young, but as mortality rates have fallen, a greater proportion of parental deaths have occurred when the children have already reached adulthood. Consequently, the most important effect on family life of any further fall in death rates will be to extend the "empty nest" stage of marriage after the children leave home. One of the most important effects of the rise in divorce, on the other hand, is to increase the proportion of parents whose marriage is dissolved while their children are still at home. According to 1973 data analyzed by Larry Bumpass and Ronald R. Rindfuss, 17 percent of children born between 1968 and 1970 experienced a disrupted family by age five, as against only 11 percent of children born between 1956 and 1958. Overall, one-third of all white children and three-fifths of all black children born between 1970 and 1973 will experience family disruption by age sixteen if the rates of 1973 continue to hold.[34]

Most of these disruptions result, at least temporarily, in a one-parent family consisting of a mother and her children, because mothers keep custody of their children in most instances. Among all children not living with two parents in 1979, 75 percent were living with their mother, only 7 percent with the father, and most of the rest with other relatives.[35] As marital disruption increased in the 1970s, so did the number of one-parent families headed by women. In 1979, 5.3 million women headed families that included their own children under eighteen, an increase of 81 percent since 1970.[36] About two-thirds of the rise between 1970 and 1979 was caused by the increased number of divorced and separated mothers. (The remainder was caused by an increase in the number of never-married mothers.) Earlier in the century, it was common for divorcing parents to send their children to live with relatives or for divorced mothers to take their children and move in with kin. Today, however, most currently divorced mothers live alone with their children.[37] Half of the children in one-parent families formed by marital disruption will spend more than four years in this type of family before their mother remarries or they turn eighteen.[38] Much has been written about the social and economic situation of parents and children in one-parent families, and I discuss the consequences of living in such a family in later chapters.

Separation. One other form of marital dissolution to be considered is separation. Most married couples stop living together before they are legally divorced. Some remain separated—without divorcing—for an extended period or even for the rest of their lives. Others separate and then reconcile their differences and resume their marriages. Even for couples who eventually divorce, the process of moving into separate households may be more difficult and traumatic than subsequently obtaining a divorce. Unfortunately, very little is known about separation. Unlike marriage and divorce, which are always sanctioned by the state, many separations are informal arrangements between two spouses. Consequently, official records on legal separations, which are incomplete in any case, give an inadequate picture of the number of separations. We don't know how many separations occur each year, nor do we have satisfactory information on the average duration of the period between separation and divorce. Needless to say, our knowledge of the trends in separation in recent decades is minimal. Because separation is closely associated with divorce, it can be assumed that as the divorce rate has risen, so has the rate of separation; but we can't go much beyond this simple generalization.

The Bureau of the Census does provide annual information in its Current Population Survey on the number of people who were separated from their spouses at the time of the survey, but the figures are difficult to interpret for two reasons. First, the number of people currently separated depends not only on the rate at which people become separated but also on the rate at which they stop being separated—that is, on how quickly they divorce or reconcile once they have separated. As a result, the number of people currently separated could increase over time merely because separated spouses were taking more time to obtain their divorces, even if the overall rate of divorce were decreasing. Second, demographers suspect that the category "currently separated" is not accurately reported in surveys. The 1970 census, for example, reported the following impossible situation: 1,317,620 women said they were separated from their husbands, but only 873,471 men admitted that they were separated from their wives.[39] It seems likely that some of the so-called separated women had never married their supposed husbands and that some men who actually were separated from their wives reported instead that they had never married.

A few surveys of the childbearing experiences of women under forty-five have collected information on the dates of past separations as well as past divorces. James McCarthy, who analyzed data from the 1973 National Survey of Family Growth, found strong racial differences involving separation. Within ten years of their first marriage, about four out of ten black women and two out of ten white women would separate, if the levels of separation reported in the 1973 survey continued. Once they separate, black women seem to take longer to obtain a divorce than do white women; five years after their separation begins, about half of all separated black women are still separated, compared to only about one-tenth of all the white women.[40] As a result of this higher probability of separation and longer duration to divorce, at any one time a far greater proportion of black women are currently separated than are white women. In 1979, for instance, 15 percent of all black women aged twenty-five to forty-four were currently separated, as against 3 percent of all white women of that age.[41] These figures might be biased, however, if black and white women differ in their tendencies to incorrectly report themselves as separated. Since 1960 the rate of increase in the proportion currently separated actually has been greater for whites than for blacks, but the large racial difference still remains.[42] I return to the topic of black-white differences in marital status in chapter 4.

REMARRIAGE AFTER DIVORCE

Remarriages have been common in the United States since its beginnings, but until this century almost all remarriages followed widowhood. In the Plymouth Colony about one-third of all men and one-quarter of all women who lived full lifetimes remarried after the death of a spouse, but there was little divorce.[43] Even as late as the 1920s, brides and grooms who were remarrying were more likely to have been widowed than divorced.[44] Since then, however, the increase in divorce and the decline in mortality have altered the balance: by 1978, 87 percent of all brides who were remarrying were previously divorced, and 13 percent were widowed. For grooms who were remarrying in 1978, 89 percent were divorced.[45] Thus it is only in recent decades that remarriage after divorce has become the predominant form of remarriage. And since the turn of the century, such remarriages have increased as a proportion of all marriages. In 1900 only 3 percent of all brides—including both the single and the previously married—were divorced. In 1930 9 percent of all brides were divorced, and in 1978, 28 percent of all brides were divorced.[46]

Part of this increase in remarriage is caused simply by the greater proportion of divorced people in the general population. In addition, a greater proportion of divorced people remarry each year today than earlier in the century. In 1920 and again in 1940, about 100 out of every 1,000 divorced and widowed women aged fourteen to fifty-four remarried each year, but by the late 1960s the remarriage rate had jumped to more than 150 per 1,000. Although the rate has since dropped to 134 per 1,000 in the period 1975 to 1977, it is still considerably above earlier levels.[47] The recent decline in the annual remarriage rates may mean that fewer divorced people will remarry in the future, but it also may reflect only a postponement of remarriage.

The upshot of all this is that most people who get divorced remarry. About five out of six men and about three out of four women remarry after a divorce, according to the experiences of the older generations alive today. And those who are going to remarry do so soon after their divorce: about half of all remarriages take place within three years after divorce. In addition, the average age at which people remarry appears to have declined somewhat during the century. Women born in 1910 to 1914 who remarried following divorce had a median age of about thirty-five when they remarried; for young adults in the 1970s and early 1980s, that median will probably be about thirty.[48]

When either partner in a remarriage has children from a previous marriage, the structure of the new family can be quite complex. It may include children from the wife's previous marriage, from the husband's previous marriage, and from the new marriage. The children from previous marriages often create links between the household of the remarried parent and the household of that parent's ex-spouse. Stepgrandparents and other quasi-kin may play important roles in the lives of the parents and children. Not all families of remarriages, of course, exhibit the full range of complexity, but more of these families now have stepchildren; the percentage of divorces that involve children has increased during the postwar years.[49] In 1978, 10 million children lived in a household with one natural parent and one stepparent. These children constituted one out of every eight children living in a two-parent family.[50]

Conventional wisdom suggests that remarriages should be more successful than first marriages because of the greater maturity and experience of the partners, but the divorce rate suggests otherwise. A number of studies have shown a modestly greater risk of marital disruption for remarriages after divorce than for first marriages.[51] According to recent estimates by the National Center for Health Statistics, 67 out of every 100 first marriages begun in 1975 would survive to their tenth anniversary if 1975 divorce and death probabilities continued to hold, while only 52 out of every 100 remarriages would survive for ten years. Part of this difference is a result of the greater risk of death for remarried persons, who tend to be older than persons in first marriages. But even when the risk of dying is taken into account, the results are similar: if no one died during the first ten years of their marriage, 30 percent of all first marriages and 39 percent of all remarriages begun in 1975 would end in divorce within ten years, according to the NCHS projections.[52]

Some researchers have linked this higher probability of divorce to the complex family structures of remarriages, while others have argued that the first-married and remarried populations differ in personal characteristics that could influence the risk of divorce. In either case, the expanded families of remarriages after divorce may complicate the lives of remarried adults and their children. In later chapters, I explore the consequences of this increasingly common form of family life.

AN OVERVIEW

The indicators I have reviewed show that in attempting to summarize the changes in marriage, divorce, and remarriage since World War II, it is important to choose our frame of reference with care. We often contrast the situation of the 1950s with that of the 1970s, implicitly assuming that the 1950s were representative of family life throughout the first half of the century. Thus we sometimes conclude that the family patterns of the 1970s differ sharply overall from what was experienced in the past. But as I have shown in this chapter, this sweeping conclusion is unwarranted; in many respects it is the 1950s that stand out as more unusual.

During that decade the men and women born and raised during the depression and the war years came of age. They married sooner than any other cohorts who have reached adulthood in the twentieth century before or since. About three-fourths of the women born in 1930 to 1934 were married by age twenty-three; in contrast, women born twenty years before or later were two or three years older when three-fourths of them had married. Moreover, the long-term rise in divorce affected those who came of age in the 1950s less than some other cohorts. In addition, more of the women in the parental generation of the 1950s had two or more children than did the women in either their parents' or, it appears, their children's generations. The distinctive family patterns of the young adults of the 1950s suggest that when we look for explanations of the postwar trends, we should examine the experience of growing up in the depression and the war years, as I do in the next chapter.

As for the children of the parental generation of the 1950s—who were born during the baby boom and who reached adulthood in the 1960s and 1970s—they, too, have been distinctive in some respects. To be sure, their pattern of marrying has been more like the typical twentieth-century pattern than was the case for their parents' generation. But the lifetime levels of divorce for the children of the baby boom are likely to increase beyond what we would expect from the long-term trend. If current rates hold for the next ten to twenty years, about half of all the marriages begun in the mid-1970s will end in divorce. Most of those who divorce will also remarry, creating an unprecedented number of marriages in which one or both spouses has been previously married. In chapter 3 I explore the consequences for adults and children of this increase in divorce and remarriage.

2
The Explanations

Each change in family life since the depression seems to have taken scholars by surprise. The dismal employment situation of the 1930s forced single people to postpone marrying and forced married couples to postpone having children. Worried experts warned that the low rate of births, if sustained, would lead to a drastic decrease in population. In 1933 a presidential panel predicted that the American population would peak at between 145 and 190 million and then decline.[1] Today it stands at more than 226 million and is still rising. Even as late as the end of World War II, respected demographers were sticking to their pessimistic projections.

What no one foresaw was the postwar baby boom. The young men and women of the late 1940s and 1950s married earlier and had children faster than did their parents' generation. Observers of family life in the 1950s, somewhat taken aback by this sudden shift, looked around for explanations. Some commentators proposed that in the aftermath of depression and war, Americans had begun to place a higher value on marriage, children, and home life. Yet it was often unclear from their writings how and why this tendency had developed. In any case, during the 1960s the divorce rate began to rise very steeply, fertility fell once again, and young adults again postponed marrying.

From the vantage point of the 1980s, it is possible to see in these ups and downs some patterns of cause and effect that may have been difficult to discern ten or twenty years ago. New scholarship has suggested ways in which historical circumstances have shaped trends in family life since the depression, although there still is disagreement among scholars about the causes of the trends, and the disagreement becomes more pronounced the closer we look to the present. It is possible, nevertheless, to draw some reasonable conclusions about the forces behind the trends in marriage, divorce, and remarriage since World War II. And, because of the close connection between trends in fertility and in marital formation and dissolution, I also examine the reasons for the rise and fall of the birth rate.

As chapter 1 showed, the generation that came of age after World War II differed from generations before or since in its pattern of marrying, divorcing, and childbearing. This difference suggests two possible explanations for the trends of the 1950s. First, the attitudinal climate or the economic situation of that decade may have differed from other periods in ways that encouraged young men and women to marry and have children. Second, some shared set of childhood and adolescent experiences, some special characteristics these cohorts carried with them into adulthood, may have influenced their behavior in the 1950s.

THE 1950s

After nearly a decade of depression and four terrible years of war, Americans finally had prosperity as they entered the 1950s. And, except for the more limited Korean conflict, they finally had peace. Millions of men and women had been forced to postpone marrying during the hard times of the 1930s and the austerity and separation brought about by the war. It was not surprising, then, that they married in record numbers in the late 1940s and that the birth rate soon rose dramatically. What was surprising was that years after this pent-up demand for marriage and children should have been satisfied, the birth and marriage rates remained high. As late as 1956, the Bureau of the Census estimated that nearly half of all young women who would ever marry would do so before they reached age twenty.[2] Moreover, the annual birth rate rose steadily in the 1950s, reaching its peak in 1957. Had the birth rate remained at the 1957 level, the average woman would have given birth to about four children before the end of her childbearing years.[3] (In fact, the birth rate fell sharply in the 1960s and 1970s.)

Looking back now to the 1950s, we can see how unusual this pattern of marriage and childbearing was. What produced this surprising turn of events? One common explanation is that there was a general shift in Americans' attitudes toward marriage and childbearing, a shift that caused many young adults to begin forming their families sooner. Nearly all accounts of the 1950s stress the great importance attached to home, family, and children. Many popular commentators ascribed this shift to what they saw as a great national exhaustion: emotionally drained from their battles against an economic collapse and a monstrous enemy, Americans supposedly shunned the great issues of the day and retreated into their personal lives.[4] Indeed, widely read authors and commentators and well-known political leaders in the 1950s all extolled the virtues of a traditional family life. Women's magazines published a steady stream of articles praising the homemaker and warning women of the perils of trying to combine marriage and childrearing with work outside the home. Adlai Stevenson, in a famous address to the graduates of Smith College in 1955, advised them that their place in politics was to "influence man and boy" through the "humble role of housewife."

And nowhere, according to the popular view, was the increased emphasis on home and family more noticeable than in the expanding suburbs. With the help of government-guaranteed mortgages, millions of families purchased single-family homes beyond the borders of the cities. The family-centered life in the suburbs came under sharp attack from social critics. The new suburban communities, according to the critics, were centered around children and run by the mothers. The long commute to work, they said, kept husbands away from early in the morning until night. Meanwhile, the mothers supposedly were engaged in an endless round of activities on behalf of their children, chauffeuring them to nursery school, ballet lessons, and Little League games.[5]

Yet it is easy to exaggerate the extent and importance of the attitudinal shift in the 1950s and the family-centered style of life. At the same time that the media were annoucing a shift toward traditional values, more and more married women were taking jobs outside the home. Moreover, many commentators in the 1950s talked about the four- or five-child family, as if families this large had once again become common. But we now know that there was not a return to large families in the 1950s. Much of the increase in the annual birth rates can be traced to two developments: a greater proportion of young women had at least two children, and women tended to have their children sooner after they married. There was also an increase in the proportion of women who had three or four children, but there appears to have been a decrease in the proportion who had more than four.[6] The prevailing image of life in the suburbs was based on studies of only one type—the upper-middle-class suburbs surrounding major cities. By the early 1960s scholars were discovering much more diversity in suburbs than the critics had contended; not all resembled a Westchester County exurb full of advertising executives who commuted to Manhattan. In working-class and lower-middle-class suburbs—which did not receive as much attention from social critics and the media—life did not appear to be much different from working-class and lower-middle-class city neighborhoods.[7] This discovery cast doubt upon many of the stereotypes of suburbia promulgated by its critics in the 1950s.

Nevertheless, attitudes toward personal life in the 1950s probably did differ to some degree from attitudes in the preceding and succeeding decades. Historian John Modell, for instance, reported that in a 1957 opinion poll Americans gave as an "ideal" age for getting married a younger age than was given in 1946 or 1974 polls.[8] Yet it doesn't necessarily follow that the change in attitudes caused people to change their behavior. Rather, it may have been that young people changed both their attitudes and their behaviors at about the same time in response to other developments. Modell suggested that the postwar economic boom was the stimulus for the changes: the better job market made it easier for young couples to marry, and this lessening of constraints influenced people to reconsider—and often lower—their estimate of the ideal age at which to marry.[9]

In some cases attitudinal change may have occurred well after the associated behavioral change. As I show later in this chapter, changes in attitudes toward women working—a related dimension of people's values about family life—appear to have lagged well behind changes in women's work behavior. In fact, there is little evidence to support (or refute) the popular belief that a society-wide change in attitudes brought about the family patterns of the 1950s. It is a theory that seems to make sense to many people who lived through the period, but it is difficult to demonstrate whether the shift was a cause or an effect of changing patterns of marriage and childbearing.

If a general shift in attitudes were the only explanation proposed for the trends of the 1950s, I would be more inclined to overlook its shortcomings. There is, however, another explanation, which emphasizes the lasting effects of the childhood and adolescent experiences common to the cohorts born in the 1920s and 1930s.

Growing up in the depression often meant belonging to a family in which the father was unable to find steady work—or in many cases, any work at all. When the father was unemployed, the family's income plummeted, and wives and teenage children, especially teenage boys, were forced to get a job if they could. A man who had been a reliable breadwinner before the depression might watch helplessly as his wife and children became the family's only wage earners. In this situation the father lost not only his income but also his authority. Mirra Komarovsky reported on the breakdown of the unemployed father's status at home in her classic study, *The Unemployed Man and his Family*. She wrote about one man who had been on relief for three years:

> Mr. Brady says that while the children don't blame him for his unemployment, he is sure that they don't think as much about the old man as they used to. "It's only natural. When a father cannot support his family, supply them with clothing and good food, the children are bound to lose respect."[10]

Mr. Brady's seventeen-year-old son Henry was the only employed member of the family, earning $12 per week. He told Komarovsky:

"I'm my own boss now. Nobody can tell me what to do or how to spend my money. Working makes you feel independent. I remind them who makes the money. They don't say much. They just take it, that's all. *I'm* not the one on relief. I can't help feeling that way."

Henry said that seeing his father so discouraged and without ambition made him lose respect for him. "He is not the same father, that's all. You can't help not looking up to him like we used to."[11]

Once, when the family was almost finished with dinner, Henry walked in. There were no extra chairs, so Mr. Brady got up and relinquished his seat to his son. Henry took his father's place at the table in a matter-of-fact way, as if it were his due.

Did the experiences of Henry Brady and other adolescents from homes hit hard by the depression influence their later patterns of marriage and family life? One scholar who has begun to answer this question is sociologist Glen H. Elder, Jr. His study of children born in Oakland, California, in 1920 and 1921, *Children of the Great Depression,* traces the long-term effects of the depression on some of the children who grew up during it.[12] The Oakland Growth Study, as it was originally called, was begun in 1932 as a study of the physical, intellectual, and social development of 167 children who were then eleven years old. The researchers reinterviewed these subjects periodically until the mid-1960s. Elder divided the subjects into middle-class and working-class groups, and he also divided them into "deprived" and "nondeprived" groups. Persons were considered deprived if their families had suffered an income loss of more than 35 percent between 1929 and 1933. By this criterion, slightly more than half of the middle-class children and about two-thirds of the working-class children were classified as living in deprived homes.

Elder demonstrated how independence increased and what the consequences of this were for adolescent boys. When Oakland families were hit by the depression, teenage sons were sent to work to help compensate for their fathers' lost earnings. The sons' incomes increased their independence from parental control, as Komarovsky showed in the case of Henry Brady, and their jobs gave the boys a chance to extend their network of friends and acquaintances. They often became more actively involved with their peers, they went out on school nights, they dated earlier.

While the boys were sent to work, their sisters were required to help more around the house. According to the Oakland study, girls from families that had suffered a large loss of income did more domestic chores than girls from more fortunate families. Consequently, at an early age girls became heavily involved with the tasks that make up the traditional adult female role of homemaker or housewife. In addition, according to Elder, deprived families were marked by a more distant and dissonant relationship between father and daughter. He characterized the overall experiences of the deprived boys and girls during the 1930s as "the downward extension of adultlike experience." Boys became more involved in the kind of work adult males typically do, and girls took on more of the work adult women typically do.

Most of the Oakland children married during or just after the war and had their first child soon thereafter. Women from the deprived families, Elder found, married earlier and placed a higher value on family activities—as opposed to work, leisure, or community activities—than did women from the nondeprived families. Among the deprived women, Elder believes, the distant relationships with their fathers and the stronger socialization for the role of homemaker led to an earlier age at marriage. The Oakland men from deprived families also valued family life highly, particularly the chance to have and rear children.

In general, family life was more highly valued among those Oakland men and women whose families had suffered most from the effects of the depression while they were growing up. Perhaps, as Elder suggested, these children of the depression came to view strong families as valuable resources that were all the more desirable because of their scarcity during the years of economic hardship. Perhaps children were seen as a wise investment by men and women who had seen their own parents subsist only with the aid of the money that children brought home. Or perhaps the absence of a warm, loving relationship between the father, on the one hand, and the mother and children led some of these children to build their own secure family relationships as soon as they could. Whatever the precise mechanism, the Oakland study leaves little doubt that the experience of growing up in a deprived family during the depression influenced the attitudes of men and women toward marriage, family, and children.

These attitudes and values may have affected the trends in family life that occurred when those who grew up in the depression were young adults in the late 1940s and the 1950s. An earlier age at marriage, a greater proportion ever marrying, a higher birth rate, and a stable divorce rate all are consistent with the social-psychological effects outlined by Elder and other students of the depression. Even a study as intensive as Elder's, however, doesn't firmly establish the connection between attitudes and subsequent behavior. Moreover, it is possible that the men and women in the Oakland sample were different somehow from most others born in the early 1920s. Yet the study, with its thirty-year scope and detailed information, creates the strong impression that the trends of the 1950s may well have evolved, in part, from the experience of being a child of the Great Depression.

Elder and other sociologists who have studied depression life have emphasized the social-psychological effects of economic hardship; economist Richard A. Easterlin has also considered the demographic effects.[13] As I described above, the birth rate dropped during the 1920s and then plunged even lower during the depression, to the point that some eminent demographers predicted that the United States population would soon decline. The relatively small size of the cohorts born in the 1920s and 1930s at first made little difference in their lives; but according to Easterlin, this factor was later a distinct advantage. For as it turned out, these men and women had the good fortune to begin to marry and to have children in the late 1940s, when the American economy started its sustained postwar boom. The demand for young workers was high, and because of the small size of these cohorts, the supply was low. This imbalance made it easier for young adult males to find a satisfactory job. By and large, their earnings were high compared to those of young men during the depression.

Even the relatively good employment picture in the 1950s, though, didn't necessarily ensure that couples would marry younger and that births would increase. It could have happened, Easterlin points out, that single young men would spend their larger paychecks on themselves and that young couples would use all of their extra money to buy bigger houses, more furniture, and the like. That they didn't do so, he contends, was the result of one of the psychological effects of growing up in the depression. A person's standard of living, Easterlin maintains, is determined by the material conditions he or she experiences during childhood and especially during adolescence. Consequently the children who grew up during the scarcity of the depression developed a modest taste for material goods. When they reached adulthood, the favorable employment situation for young men meant that they could marry, satisfy their desires for material goods, and still have money left over to cover the costs of having and raising children. Thus their relatively favorable employment situation, in conjunction with the modest material standards these men developed while growing up, resulted in a trend toward earlier marriage and more childbearing. In addition, the same favorable situation led to less conflict between spouses and a smaller rise in the divorce rate than the long-term trend would have indicated.

Easterlin's explanation for the trends of the 1950s is consistent with the implications that can be drawn from Elder's work. Both believe that the experience of growing up in the depression influenced people's values in important ways. Elder points to the greater emphasis on family and children; Easterlin notes the development of a modest standard of living. To these psychological effects, Easterlin adds the effect of belonging to a small cohort: better job opportunities.

Yet at least one difficulty arises when we use these cohort-based explanations to account for the trends of the 1950s. As Elder's study suggests, and as Easterlin has noted, the psychological impact of the depression probably was stronger for adolescents than for younger children. Komarovsky made a similar distinction: many of the unemployed fathers in her sample appeared to lose authority over their teenaged children, but they were more likely to report an improvement than a deterioration in their relationships with children under twelve.[14] Those who were teenagers during the depression years, of course, had to have been born by the early 1920s. It is unlikely that the lives of children born in the 1930s—who reached adolescence after the war—were touched by the depression in the same way as the Oakland cohort of 1920–1921. The cohorts of the 1930s were too young to have shared fully in the downward extension of adultlike experience, and they may have been too young to have had their standard of living influenced by the hardship around them. Thus we cannot easily extend Elder's analysis to the men and women born in the 1930s, nor can we assume that they developed a modest taste for material goods. Yet when the cohorts of the 1930s reached adulthood in the 1950s they continued, and even advanced, the trend toward earlier marriage and faster childbearing.

Elder's study of men and women born in the early 1920s, therefore, helps us to understand the behavior of only some members of the parental generation of the 1950s. And Easterlin's model also works better for people who were born in the 1920s than for those born in the 1930s. Still, an important part of Easterlin's model does apply more generally: both the 1920s and the 1930s cohorts were small in size; in fact, the number of births was lower in the early and mid-1930s than in the 1920s. If relative cohort size influenced the marriage and childbearing pattern of young adults independently of material aspirations, then Easterlin's explanation may apply to most of the new parents of the 1950s.

In sum, I have described two explanations for the trends of the 1950s. Partisans of the first explanation claim that there was a society-wide change in attitudes about home and family in that decade, a change that was either a reaction to the disruption of war or a consequence of postwar prosperity or both. The altered climate of opinion, according to this view, encouraged young adults to marry and to begin having children. The scholars who have developed the second explanation emphasize the distinctiveness of the cohorts coming of age in the 1950s. They point to the long-term effects of growing up during the depression on people's values and to the relatively favorable labor market position that the small cohort size ensured.

These two perspectives correspond to two general types of explanation for change over time in human behavior—"period" and "cohort" explanations. Period explanations refer to the consequences of events that occur during the period studied. The view that patterns of marriage and childbearing changed as a result of a contemporaneous, society-wide shift in values can be considered a period explanation of the 1950s trends. Cohort explanations refer to the consequences in later life of the early experiences or shared characteristics of particular birth cohorts. The view that the psychological impact of growing up in the depression—or the size of one's cohort—influenced one's later family life can be considered a cohort explanation for the trends of the 1950s. Since each cohort lives in a different period and therefore is subject to a different set of period-based influences, it is difficult to determine whether social change from generation to generation is produced by the differing characteristics of the cohorts involved or by society-wide changes during the time period studied. Period-based and cohort-based effects, in other words, are often confounded.[15]

It may well be that accounting for the trends of the 1950s requires giving credence to both period and cohort explanations. Easterlin and Elder have tried with some success to place their cohort-based arguments on a firmer empirical foundation than have the advocates of period-based explanations.[16] But I have noted the limitations of trying to explain all of the changes in marriage and childbearing using just the cohort based approach. Moreover, much of the evidence for Easterlin's model rests on inspection of the relationships among national trends in relative cohort size, birth rates, unemployment rates, and the like. Research on the behavior of individuals over time offers less support for his thesis; one recent study of a group of high school seniors who were followed for several years found little evidence that their income position, relative to their parents' income, influenced their timing of marriage and childbearing.[17] In addition, I don't believe we can ignore the many reports of a widespread change in values among adults of all ages in the 1950s. Nor can we overlook the evidence that changes in marriage and childbearing during the 1950s occurred not only among the cohorts born in the 1920s and 1930s but among older Americans as well. The annual rate of childbearing also increased in the 1950s for women who were in their mid- to late thirties or early forties.[18] I would argue that both the period- and cohort-based effects were operating and that, in fact, they reinforced each other, thus strengthening the trends of the 1950s. The childhood and adolescent experiences of many of the men and women born in the 1920s predisposed them to place a greater value on home and family and, possibly, a lower value on material comforts; when the general shift in values about family life occurred in the 1950s, they may have been in the vanguard. Moreover, the small size of the cohorts of the 1920s and 1930s worked to their advantage during the postwar economic boom. Their relatively favorable economic situation, in turn, may have made it easier for them to achieve the kind of family life they desired.

From all of the studies reviewed here, one gains the impression that the lives of the men and women born in the 1920s and 1930s were shaped by a series of events beyond their control. The depression brought the older among them economic hardship as children, but it also provided many with experiences that proved valuable later in life. For instance, Elder found evidence that middle-class men from deprived families were more successful in their careers than were middle-class men from nondeprived homes. After the war, in which many of the men fought, and some died, came the postwar economic boom, which finally brought a change in these people's luck. It provided the prosperity that allowed them to satisfy their desire for stability at work and at home. One result of this remarkable sequence of events was the trends in marriage, divorce, and childbearing that marked the 1950s.

THE 1960s AND 1970s

In explaining the trends in family life after 1960—the rising divorce rate, the rising age at marriage, the declining birth rate —some observers stress the effects of the increase in young married women who work outside the home, others point to the tougher economic situation facing young men, others note improvements in contraception, and still others write about the decline of traditional attitudes toward women's roles, marriage, and divorce. It is difficult to either reject any of these explanations out of hand or to give any of them full credit for producing the recent trends. In this section I consider the major explanations and the criticisms that have been raised against them.

First, to resolve a prior question, is there anything to explain? So far, I have emphasized the distinctiveness of family life in the 1950s. By extension, one could argue that the reversals of those trends in the 1960s represented a return to the usual historical pattern: young adults once again married later, the divorce rate resumed its long-term rise, and the birth rate resumed its long-term fall. This line of reasoning, carried to its logical conclusion, might suggest that there is no need to explain the trends of the 1960s and 1970s at all, except in terms of modernization, the growth and development of capitalist societies, or some such long-term perspective. Many demographers, in fact, do argue that the declining birth rate of the 1960s and 1970s should be thought of as consistent with long-term developments in our society. For example, Charles F. Westoff wrote:[19]

Every time the birthrate records a new low (frequently in recent years) a demographer received inquiries from journalists about what the decline can be attributed to: "the pill," abortion, sterilization, recession, the women's movement or some other ad hoc explanation. To ask what caused the latest decline, however, is to ask the wrong question. The decline is the long-term reality. The birthrate has been coming down more or less steadily for the past 200 years in this country—with the exception of one period. The real question, and the more perplexing one, is what caused that exception: the baby boom that lasted for more than a decade after World War II.

The view that the 1960s and 1970s represented a return to more typical patterns of marriage and childbearing, although contrary to conventional wisdom, does help us understand some of the recent developments in family life. Yet it clearly will not suffice as an explanation of all that has occurred. On the one hand, the indicators reviewed in chapter 1 showed that in the 1960s and 1970s the timing of first marriage did become more consistent with the patterns prevalent before World War II. Consequently, there is no historical basis for claiming, as some observers have, that the recent trend toward later marriage reflects widespread disenchantment with the institution of marriage. But on the other hand, chapter 1 showed that the rise in divorce in the 1960s and 1970s exceeded the increase we would expect on the basis of the long-term trend over the past hundred years. The recent rise in divorce is unprecedented in the speed with which the rate increased; it cannot be accounted for simply by appealing to the march of history. Moreover, even though the timing of marriage is now consistent with the timing in the earlier decades of the century, the reasons why people marry at an older age now may well differ from the reasons why they did so in the early 1900s.

Attitudinal Change. We need to examine more specific explanations for recent developments, especially for the one that has caused the most concern, the rise in divorce. One explanation is that in recent years people have become more tolerant of divorce, making it easier for persons in unhappy marriages to leave their spouses. According to this view, much of the stigma previously associated with being a divorced person has faded; a divorce is no longer seen as a mark of failure or disgrace. Consequently, married persons are said to be more likely to resort to divorce than they were a few decades ago.

That attitudes toward divorce have changed in recent years is undoubtedly true, but we don't have much information about the timing of this change or about its effect on people's behavior. What little we do know suggests that attitudes did not begin to change noticeably until sometime after the mid-1960s or perhaps as late as the early 1970s. In 1945 and again in 1966, national samples of adults were asked if they thought that the divorce laws in their states were too strict or not strict enough. As Figure 2-1 demonstrates, the most popular response in 1945 was "not strict enough," and virtually the same proportion of people gave this response in 1966 as in 1945. In addition, there was a modest, 4 percentage-point increase in those saying "too strict," between 1945 and 1966, but the largest changes were a decrease in those saying "about right" and an increase in those saying they didn't know. These results suggest that between 1945 and 1966 attitudes toward divorce changed slowly, although there may have been fluctuations during the intervening two decades that these two surveys cannot reflect.

Since the mid-1960s, however, there appears to have been substantial attitudinal change. In 1968, 1974, and 1978 national

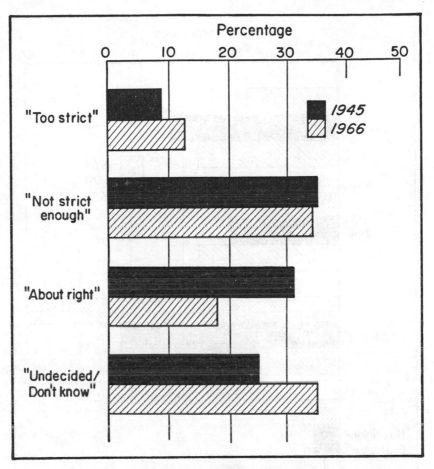

Figure 2-1 Attitudes toward divorce laws, 1945 and 1966. 1945: "Do you think the divorce laws in your state are now too strict or not strict enough?" 1966: "Generally speaking, would you say divorce laws in this state are too strict or not strict enough?" (Sources: American Institute of Public Opinion, Study 341 [1945] and 723 [1966]. 1945 data published in "The Quarter's Polls," *Public Opinion Quarterly* 9 [Summer 1945]: 233. 1966 data published in Gallup Opinion Index, report no. 9, Feb. 1966, p. 21.)

samples of adults were asked if they thought that divorce in this country should be easier or more difficult to obtain than it is now. Between 1968 and 1974, as Figure 2-2 shows, the percentage responding "easier" rose by 14 percentage points and the percentage responding "more difficult" dropped by 17 percentage points. Thus sometime between 1968 and 1974 more adults began to favor the easier granting of divorce. Between 1974

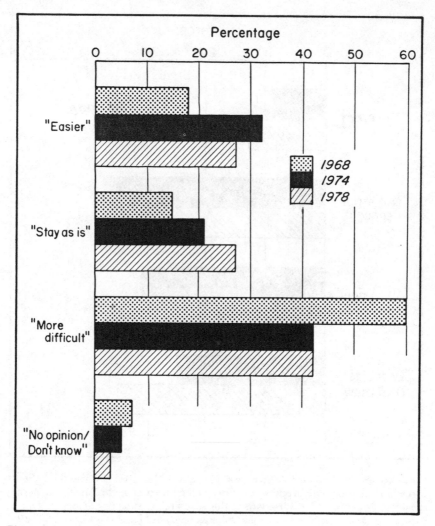

Figure 2-2 Attitudes toward divorce, 1968, 1974, and 1978: "Should divorce in this country be easier or more difficult to obtain than it is now?" (Sources: for 1968, American Institute for Public Opinion, Study 764, data published in Gallup Opinion Index, report no. 41, Nov. 1968; for 1974 and 1978, National Opinion Research Center, General Social Surveys.)

and 1978 the percentage responding "easier" fell somewhat, and the proportion responding "stay as is" rose correspondingly. This latter change doesn't necessarily indicate a hardening of attitudes toward divorce since 1974; rather, it may reflect people's responses to the introduction in the 1970s of no-fault divorce laws, which did make divorce easier to obtain in most states.

As I showed in chapter 1, the recent rise in divorce began in the early 1960s. Yet according to the sparse survey evidence just reviewed, widespread changes in attitudes may not have begun until the end of the 1960s or the early 1970s. It may be, then, that changes in attitudes toward divorce followed changes in divorce behavior. I suspect that changes in attitudes were not an important cause of the initial rise in divorce in the 1960s and, in fact, that the rise in divorce may have prompted people to begin to reassess their attitudes. Once attitudes toward divorce began to change markedly—probably at the start of the 1970s, give or take a few years—then the shift in people's beliefs may have provided a new stimulus for further rises in divorce. But if we are seeking an initial force behind the recent rise in divorce, we should look elsewhere.

More than half of the states enacted some form of no-fault divorce legislation in the 1970s, beginning with California in 1970.[20] These laws, which make the process of divorcing easier and less stigmatizing, are another indication of the recent liberalization of attitudes toward divorce. Some observers suggested that the changes in the law would spur even more couples to divorce, but state divorce statistics for the 1970s do not support this contention. Divorce rates in most no-fault states were no higher in the 1970s than would be expected from the trend in the states that did not reform their laws.[21] The spread of no-fault divorce laws seems to have been a reaction to changing attitudes and to the increase in divorce, not a stimulus to more divorce.

Married Women in the Labor Force. A more promising line of inquiry centers on the changes in women's roles. One of the long-term trends that scholars associate with advanced industrial societies is an increase in the proportion of married women who are employed outside the home. In the United States the employment of married women rose sharply after World War II. Since the 1960s the greatest increase has occurred among younger married women, who are subject to a greater risk of divorce than are older women. (Half of all divorces occur within seven years of marriage.[22]) The parallel increases in the employment of younger married women and in divorce since 1960 suggest the possibility of a cause-and-effect relationship. Of course, the parallel movement of these trends could be coincidental, or both trends could be the result of some other development. What evidence is there about the significance for marriage and divorce of the changing employment patterns of women?

Social scientists study changes in the composition of the labor force, defined as all persons who are either employed or looking for work. By this definition, housewives are excluded from the labor force, even though they do productive work at home. Between 1900 and 1940 the percentage of all women who were in the labor force increased gradually, but since 1940 the percentage has risen dramatically. The rise has been especially pronounced for married women. In 1940 only one out of seven women who were currently married (with their husband present) were working outside the home or looking for work; by 1979 one out of two were working or looking for work.[23] The change was greater for married women with children—the group that had been least likely to work—than for those without children. As shown in Figure 2-3, which charts the ·labor force participation rates for married women with children in the postwar period, the rise seemed to occur in two stages. In the 1950s the rate rose faster for women with school-aged children than for women with preschool children. Then after 1960 the rate of increase was greater for women with preschool children. Between 1949 and 1959 that rate rose from 11 to 19 percent; from 1959 to 1969 it rose from 19 to 29 percent; and from 1969 to 1979 it rose from 29 to 43 percent.

A detailed discussion of the explanations that have been proposed for the movement of married women into the labor force would be beyond the scope of this book. In brief, economists such as William P. Butz and Michael P. Ward believe that the increase was caused by a postwar rise in women's wages, which increased the cost of staying home—namely, foregone earnings —to the point that many more wives sought paying jobs. According to this argument, older women, whose children already were in school, were drawn into the labor force first. Then a further rise in wages after 1960 attracted increasing numbers of

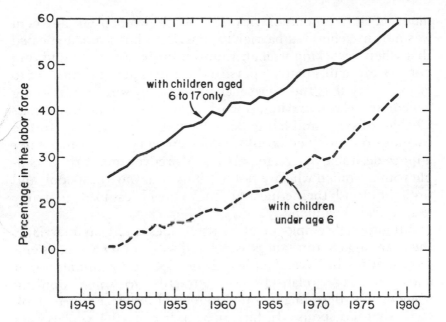

Figure 2-3 Labor force participation rates for married women with children, by age of children, 1948 to 1979. (Sources: for 1948, 1960, and 1970, U.S. Bureau of Labor Statistics, *Handbook of Labor Statistics 1978*, bulletin 2000 [1979]; for 1979, U.S. Bureau of Labor Statistics, "Multi-Earner Families Increase," Press Release no. USDL 79-747, Oct. 31, 1979.)

younger women who were caring for preschool children.[24] Sociologist Valerie K. Oppenheimer argues that the postwar rise in working women was fueled by an increase in demand for workers in the service sector of the economy, where many jobs had come to be defined as women's work. More female workers were needed to fill these jobs as teachers, secretaries, nurses, and so forth, especially with the shortage of young men in the 1950s.[25] Richard Easterlin believes the rise to be yet another manifestation of the effects of relative cohort size.[26]

More important for our purposes than the causes of the rise in the female labor force are the possible effects of this development on marital formation and dissolution. Ever since the late nineteenth century, it has been common for single young women to work for pay outside of their parents' homes. When Dreiser's Sister Carrie boarded a train for Chicago in 1889 to live with her sister and to look for a job, she was acting like many of her contemporaries. For single women employment was not, in general, a barrier to marriage, but it was expected that when a working woman found a husband, she would quit her job. Since this pattern persisted for decades, it is difficult to argue today that the mere fact of working will lead a young woman to delay marrying. A working woman might even amass a dowry of sorts, and her experience might increase her future earnings potential; either of these occurrences might make her a more desirable marriage partner. Moreover, many of the single young women who are not working today are in school, and until they finish their education, they may be less likely to marry than working women.

But although employment by itself does not delay marriage, the changing circumstances associated with young women's employment might have an effect. Better job opportunities might make marriage relatively less attractive to some working women, and they might wait longer before deciding to look seriously for a spouse. In fact, two studies of 1960 census data showed that fewer women had married in areas of the country where job opportunities for women were better, as measured by the demand in the area for jobs usually filled by women (Washington's demand was high because of its clerical work; Pittsburgh's was low because of its factory work) and by the ratio of female to male earnings.[27]

Another possibility is that as a result of the rise in labor force participation for older, married women, single young women today are more likely to believe they will be working later in life. This expectation might lead some women—especially the more educated ones—to postpone marrying while they invest time establishing themselves in the work world. I found some evidence for this hypothesis in a national sample of single women in their late teens and early twenties who were first interviewed in the late 1960s or early 1970s, then reinterviewed two years later. Other things being equal, whether a woman was working at the time of the first interview made little or no difference for whether she had married two years later. But women who said at the first interview that they planned to work at age thirty-five were, in general, less likely to have married two years later. During the period in which the study took place—1969 to 1975—

the proportion of young single women who planned to work at age thirty-five rose dramatically, especially among those with more education. Perhaps this change in expectations led some of these women to postpone marrying.[28]

As for the rise in divorce and separation, almost every well-known scholar who has addressed this topic in the twentieth century has cited the importance of the increase in the employment of women. For example, Arthur W. Calhoun, in the third volume of *A Social History of the American Family*, published in 1919, wrote that "the fact of woman's access to industry must be a prime factor in opening to her the possibility of separation from husband." Willard Waller commented in his 1938 text on the family that the employment of wives often created an opposition of interests in the family, in contrast to the interdependence found in preindustrial families. William J. Goode noted in 1963 that the possibility that a wife can support herself, even if poorly, was one of the changes that had created new alternatives to existing marriages. And more recently, Carl N. Degler argued in his comprehensive history of women and the family in America that the expanding economic opportunities for women were a necessary condition for the long-term increase in divorce. Few writers believe that women's employment is a direct cause of marital dissolution; rather, they suggest that the widening opportunities for women allow couples to separate who are unhappy with their marriages for other reasons.[29]

The employment of a wife could conceivably have quite different effects on marital stability. The earnings she brings home could ease her family's financial burden and reduce the tensions of economic hardship, thereby reducing the likelihood of marital dissolution. Or her work might bring her increased personal satisfaction, which would, in turn, improve her relationship with her husband. In the past several years a number of researchers have followed samples of married women over time to begin to sort out these effects. Most of these studies show that, other things being equal, married women who have an independent source of income are more likely to divorce or separate in the next few years. The studies also show that many other characteristics of the wife and her husband affect the probability of marital breakup, including age at marriage and the employment stability of the husband.[30] Nevertheless, it appears that on balance a woman's income reduces her dependence on her husband and makes it easier for a couple to end an unhappy marriage.

Heather L. Ross and Isabel V. Sawhill investigated marital separations among the families in the Michigan Panel Study of Income Dynamics, a national sample of families who were first interviewed in 1968 and then reinterviewed annually. Of families that had both a husband and a wife present in 1968, they found that the greater the wife's annual earnings in 1967, the greater was the probability that the family would separate by 1972. I reported similar findings from the National Longitudinal Survey of Mature Women, a national study of women aged thirty to forty-four who were first interviewed in 1967 and then reinterviewed in 1969 and 1971. Among women in the study who were married in 1967, the higher their actual or potential earnings relative to their husband's earnings, the more likely they were to separate by 1971. In an analysis of a large-scale income maintenance experiment in Seattle and Denver, Michael T. Hannan, Nancy Brandon Tuma, and Lyle P. Groeneveld found that providing a guaranteed minimum income to a family had two effects: it increased the family's total income, thereby reducing the likelihood of separation, but it also increased the wife's independence—because she was eligible for payments even if the family broke up—thereby raising the likelihood of separation. The overall effect of these two countervailing pressures depended on the level of income support provided.[31]

Most of these studies investigated the relationship of employment to marriage and divorce at the individual level. The more pertinent issue is whether an analogous relationship held at the societal level during the postwar period. From the research reviewed in this chapter, it is possible to make three statements: (1) a married woman may be more likely to divorce if she is in the labor force; (2) the labor force participation rate for younger married women rose sharply after 1960; and (3) younger married women are in general more likely to divorce than are older married women. These statements, I believe, build a plausible case that the sharp increase in young married women's participation in the labor force in the 1960s and 1970s contributed to the rise in divorce. The evidence remains circumstantial; but it seems to me that it is stronger and more suggestive than that linking any other recent trend with the rise in divorce.

The Relative Income Hypothesis. There are, however, alternative explanations for the parallel movement of young women's employment patterns, average age at marriage, and the probability of divorce. Easterlin argues that the movement of wives into the labor force and the trends in marriage and divorce after 1960 were both determined by a more fundamental trend—a decline in the income of young men relative to the income of their parents while they were growing up. As I have said, Easterlin explained the trends of the 1950s in terms of the relatively favorable income position of the young men of the small cohorts born in the 1920s and 1930s. One result of this postwar development, however, was that the next generation—the cohorts born during the late 1940s and 1950s—was very large. Easterlin contends that because the members of the baby boom cohorts grew up during a time of relative affluence, they therefore acquired a high standard of living. Unfortunately, when the large numbers of young men of the baby boom came of age in the 1960s and 1970s, they found increased competition for good jobs. Many may have had to settle for employment that offered less than they had hoped.

The situation of the cohorts of the late 1940s and 1950s, then, was the mirror image of that of the cohorts of the 1920s and 1930s, according to Easterlin: the younger cohorts had high expectations as they entered a tight labor market; the older cohorts had modest expectations as they entered a more favorable market. This relative decline in opportunity, he argues, caused the young men and women of the baby boom to marry at a later age, on the average, than did their parents' generation. The relatively unfavorable income position of the young men, combined with their tastes for material goods, meant that many young married couples postponed having children. Instead, many of the young wives went to work to supplement the family's income. In addition, he argues, increased marital conflict fueled by the tight economic situation led to the sharp increase in divorce. Easterlin doesn't rule out the possibility that the increased employment of young married women had an independent effect on marital dissolution, but he does suggest that both the increasing employment of wives and the increase in dissolution resulted ultimately from the deteriorating income position of young men.[32] Easterlin's explanation has the virtue of theoretical simplicity: he proposes the same model to account for the very different trends of the 1950s, the 1960s and 1970s, and the 1980s and beyond. By the same token, however, his explanation for the trends of the 1960s and 1970s is subject to some of the same limitations and criticisms as is his explanation for the 1950s, such as the lack of firm empirical evidence that the behavior of individuals fits his model.[33]

Improved Contraception. Aside from young women's employment and young men's economic prospects, another recent development might have affected marriage and divorce since 1960: the introduction and widespread use of better methods of contraception—notably the birth control pill, the intrauterine device, and surgical sterilization—and the greater availability of abortion. In 1960, according to surveys conducted by Norman B. Ryder and Charles F. Westoff, less than one-tenth of all couples who weren't trying to have a child were using the pill, the IUD, or sterilization; by 1970 the proportion was one-half; by 1975 it was three-fourths.[34] Yet scholars are still debating the extent to which the increased availability of better methods of birth control brought about the decline in fertility since 1960. At issue is whether fertility fell primarily because of a change in people's motivation to use birth control or primarily because of improvements in the methods available. On the one hand, Ryder and Westoff claim that much of the decline occurred simply because more effective contraceptive methods were available. On the other hand, researchers such as Judith Blake and Prithwis Das Gupta maintain that the more significant change was in people's intentions: young couples desired fewer children in the 1960s and 1970s than did their counterparts in the 1950s, as shown by public opinion surveys, and therefore, Blake and Das Gupta argue, they were more highly motivated to practice contraception.[35] Those who believe that changes in motivation are more important than changes in birth control technology note, for example, that the birth rate was low during the depression, when many couples wanted to postpone having children because of economic hardship, even though modern methods of contraception were lacking.[36]

It is even less clear how much of the post-1960 rise in age at marriage and in divorce can be attributed to the improvement in contraceptive technology and the availability of abortion. One might expect that greater control over childbearing would make it easier for married women to work outside the home, and I have shown that the increase in young married women's employment, in turn, has probably contributed to the increase in divorce. Similarly, many unmarried women may have avoided unwanted pregnancies because of the better birth control methods, thus preventing some early marriages, which have a higher probability of divorce, and possibly contributing to the rising age at marriage. Yet here again it may be that the introduction of better technology is of secondary importance compared to changes in young people's motivation to avoid or postpone having children. Some studies suggest that reduced childbearing was more a consequence than a cause of the long-term increase in young women's employment.[37] Although it is possible that improved birth control technology and easier access to abortion have had a significant, independent influence on age at marriage and on divorce, this influence has not yet been demonstrated convincingly.

The Marriage Squeeze. Demographers have noticed another development that might have caused people to postpone marriage in the 1960s and 1970s. In our society, women tend to marry men who are a few years older than they are. The young men and women who came of age in the 1960s and 1970s were born at a time of rising birth rates. Consequently, after 1960 there were more twenty-year-old women, say, than there were men aged twenty-one or twenty-two. The result of this difference in numbers, some observers believe, was a "marriage squeeze"; unable to find suitable partners, some women postponed marrying.[38] In fact, Figure 1-3 in chapter 1 showed that women tended to delay marriage more than men did in the 1960s and 1970s. In addition, Samuel Preston and Alan Richards found evidence that in 1960 in areas of the country where the sex ratio was more favorable to women, a greater proportion of them were married.[39] No one claims that the marriage squeeze accounts for all of the change in age at marriage, and few believe it has had a significant impact on the divorce rate. But it may have contributed to the increase in average age at marriage after 1960.

Summing Up. Like the explanations of the trends of the 1950s, all of these hypotheses about the trends in marriage, divorce, and childbearing in the 1960s and 1970s can be considered as either period or cohort explanations. Partisans of period explanations argue that some of the long-term changes characterizing advanced industrial societies accelerated in the United States after 1960, producing a rise in the typical age at marriage, a burst of divorce, and a sharp drop in childbearing. They emphasize the importance of the increased participation in the labor force among young married women, the development and dissemination of better contraceptive technology, or the liberalization of attitudes toward divorce. Those who subscribe to the usefulness of this general view tend to see the depression and the war as temporary interruptions, disturbances whose effects faded after the 1950s.

Scholars such as Easterlin who propose cohort explanations maintain that the depression altered patterns of marriage, divorce, and childbearing permanently—or at least for the foreseeable future. According to this view, the hard times of the depression years set in motion swings in fertility that will produce alternately large and small generations. The changes in cohort size will in turn produce in each generation swings in rates of marriage, divorce, and childbearing through such mechanisms as the relative income position of young men and the imbalance of the sex ratio for prospective marriage partners.

Why, then, were couples more likely to divorce in 1980 than in 1960, and why were they likely to have married at a later age? To some extent, the changes after 1960 represent a movement back to more typical patterns of marrying and divorcing. As I discussed in chapter 1, the average age at marriage in the 1950s was unusually low by historical standards and the lifetime probability of divorce was increasing unusually slowly. Yet the very large, post-1960 increase in divorce needs to be accounted for, and the reasons for the turnaround in age at marriage aren't obvious. By the 1970s, attitudes about divorce may have become more liberal, and this shift may have encouraged more couples to divorce. More divorce, in turn, may have stimulated a further liberalization of attitudes, and so forth, creating a kind of attitude-behavior feedback loop. But as I have argued, it is doubtful that attitudinal change was a major force in initiating the trends in the 1960s. As with the 1950s, once we consider causes other than attitudinal change, it is difficult to choose between period explanations, such as the movement of women into the labor force, or cohort explanations, such as the deteriorating economic situation of young men from large cohorts.

I would speculate that the increased labor force participation of young married women ultimately will be seen as the most important stimulus to the initial rise in age at marriage and in divorce after 1960. I have argued in this chapter that this rising participation accounted for at least part of the change, but it is impossible as yet to say precisely how large or small a part. It may be, as Easterlin suggests, that the less favorable income position of young men accounted for another part, and improved contraception and the marriage squeeze may also have contributed. Because of the general logical problem of disentangling cohort and period explanations, it is not possible to state definitely which of the effects discussed above was more important; but together they take us a long way toward accounting for the trends in marital formation and dissolution in the 1960s and 1970s.

THE 1980s

All of the explanations considered so far lead to the same conclusions about rates of marriage, divorce, and childbearing in the 1950s, 1960s, and 1970s. But these same explanations lead to contradictory predictions about the near future. At the moment, social scientists are engaged in a lively debate over what family life will be like in the 1980s.

On one side are Easterlin and other scholars with similar approaches. The drop in births in the 1960s and 1970s means that the next generation will once again be small. When they begin to enter adulthood in the 1980s, Easterlin contends, young men will once again be in short supply, as in the 1950s, and their employment opportunities will be better. Consequently, the trends will turn around again: young people will marry earlier, births will rise, and the increase in divorce will be modest. Moreover, the rate of increase of young women's labor force participation will slow, as more young married women bear children. Twenty years later, however, the situation will reverse once more, and so on, into the twenty-first century.[40] Easterlin's theory is not without its critics; it is fair to say that his view of the 1980s is the minority position. Those who argue against his predictions maintain that young women's increased participation in the labor force is a permanent phenomenon and is unlikely to abate in the 1980s, at least as long as the economy continues to grow. Because many more young married women will be working, the critics argue, the birth rate is unlikely to rise very much, and any reduction in the rate of increase in divorce will be small.[41]

Changes in Attitudes toward Women's Work. Easterlin, some of his critics contend, is mistaken in assuming that a wife's work is still seen as secondary to the husband's work, as just a supplement to the husband's earnings that can be foregone if the husband is doing well. In reply, Easterlin cites survey data on work attitudes showing, he maintains, that most women do view work as a necessary expedient rather than a valued activity in itself. In Figure 2-4 I have assembled some recent data on the work atti-

---

Figure 2-4 Attitudes toward work and family, for ever-married women less than age 45, by race, 1970 and 1977 (percentage agreeing among all who gave an opinion). *A*, "It is much better for everyone involved if the man is the achiever outside the home and the woman takes care of the home and family." *B*, "A preschool child is likely to suffer if his or her mother works." *C*, "A working mother can establish just as warm and secure a relationship with her children as a mother who does not work." (Sources: for 1970, National Fertility Survey; for 1977, National Opinion Research Center, General Social Survey.)

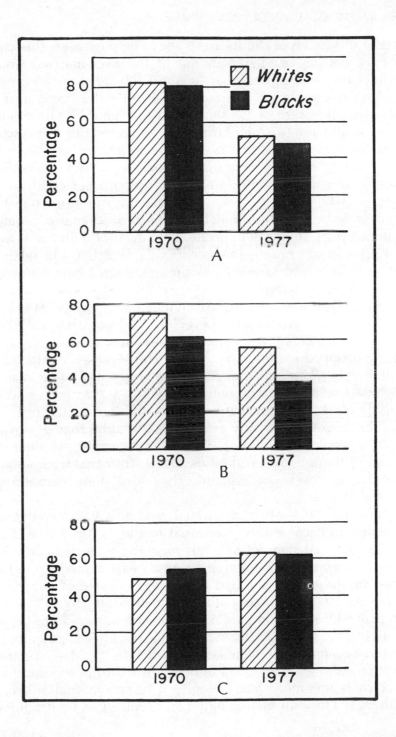

tudes of women of childbearing age to help us assess this aspect of the debate. In 1970 four out of five ever-married women under forty-five agreed that "it is much better for everyone involved if the man is the achiever outside the home and the woman takes care of the home and the family." Three out of four whites and two out of three blacks agreed that "a preschool child is likely to suffer if his or her mother works." Only half agreed with the statement that "a working mother can establish just as warm and secure a relationship with her children as a mother who does not work." Clearly, American women in 1970 tended to be quite traditional in their attitudes toward women's proper work role. These traditional attitudes didn't stop many of them from working, but something other than a belief in the desirability of working outside the home must have influenced their decisions to work.

By 1977, though, substantial change had occurred. As Figure 2-4 shows, the proportion of ever-married women of childbearing age responding traditionally to the same three survey questions dropped considerably during the seven-year interval. In 1977 only about half thought it was better if the man was the achiever, and only about half of all whites and roughly four out of ten blacks thought that preschool children suffered if their mothers worked; nearly two-thirds thought that a working mother could establish just as warm a relationship with her children. Although these responses demonstrate that traditional attitudes still were widespread, they also demonstrate rapid change.

The attitudes of men toward women's employment also seemed to become less traditional in the 1970s. In 1972 and 1978, national samples of adult men and women were asked, "Do you approve of a married woman earning money in business or industry if she had a husband capable of supporting her?" In 1972, 63 percent of men approved; in 1978 72 percent approved.[42] (The comparable figures for women were 68 percent in 1972 and 75 percent in 1978.) In addition, people's attitudes became more consistent during the 1970s—a man or woman who gave a nontraditional answer to one question on sex roles was more likely to give a nontraditional answer to others.[43] Thus, an increasingly consistent set of nontraditional attitudes seems to have emerged in the minds of more and more men and women during the 1970s.

It appears that before 1970 changes in attitudes were not nearly as rapid. Figure 2-5 displays the responses of men and women over the past forty years to survey questions about whether they would vote for a woman for president. Although this question takes us a bit far afield from female labor force participation, it is one of the few questions about women's roles that has been asked regularly for the past several decades in national surveys. There are some problems in comparing the responses over time—the exact wording of the question has varied, as have the sampling techniques of the surveys—but the general trend is probably reliable. The percentage that would vote for a woman increased gradually from the late 1930s to the late 1960s and then increased at a much faster rate through the mid-1970s. (The slowing of the increase in the late 1970s may indicate a "ceiling effect"—those who still do not approve of voting for a woman may constitute a small, vehement group

Figure 2-5 Percentage who would vote for a woman for president, by sex, 1937 to 1978. (Sources: 1937–1969, George H. Gallup, *The Gallup Poll: Public Opinion 1935–1971*, vols. 1 to 3 [New York: Random House, 1972]; for 1972–1978, National Opinion Research Center, General Social Surveys.)

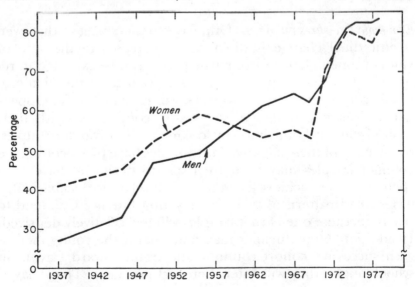

that never will approve.) If the pattern of change shown here is representative of sex-role attitudes in general, it would suggest that attitudes became more liberal only slowly and gradually before the late 1960s. Throughout most of the postwar period, then, the rising rates of female participation in the labor force seem to have coexisted with widespread traditional beliefs about women's roles.

It seems, then, that changes in attitudes about women's roles could not have been a major force behind the trends in female labor force participation, marriage, divorce, and childbearing prior to 1970. Most of the young married women who entered the labor force in the 1960s apparently went to work because they felt they needed the money. Yet the dramatic changes in attitudes since the late 1960s suggest that the greater acceptance of employment for married women may now play an independent role. It is possible, of course, that the trend in attitudes about women's roles could reverse direction in the near future, but I agree with those who believe that a sharp reversal is unlikely.[44] The spread of nontraditional attitudes may mean that more young married women will wish to remain at work; if so, any improvements in young men's economic situation will have less of an effect on trends in marriage, divorce, and childbearing.

Economic Pressures on Wives. Other researchers believe that even if attitudinal change is discounted, increases in the rate of young women's labor force participation can be expected to remain high. Valerie Oppenheimer, for instance, argues that economic pressures for wives to work will remain strong. Oppenheimer suggests that one way young couples establish their desired standard of living is by looking at slightly older couples. Since many of these slightly older couples have two incomes, the younger couples may be more likely to decide to have both spouses work to achieve a comparable level. Once established, a widespread pattern of two-earner young families may tend to persist, because one-earner couples will feel relatively deprived. In addition, Oppenheimer maintains that if the young men of each successive cohort continue the trend toward staying in school longer, they will enter their first jobs later. This delayed entry, she argues, will depress their relative earnings and lower their seniority; it will also place them in higher white collar occupations in which earnings rise more steeply with age. As a result, she claims, the net effect of increases in schooling may be to place the young men of the 1980s at a relative disadvantage compared to older men. This tendency, in turn, would make it more likely for young couples to decide that they need the wife's income.[45]

Currently, then, two groups of scholars hold contradictory views on the likely trends in marriage, divorce, and childbearing in the 1980s. In theory, the events of the next decade should provide a clear test of explanations based on cohort size versus explanations based on society-wide changes in women's roles, attitudes, or contraceptive technology. Yet it is possible that the birth rate will rise but only moderately, that age at marriage will decline but only slightly, and that the divorce rate will increase somewhat more slowly than in the past twenty years. In this event both sides could claim victory. The very early indicators do show some reversals: the crude birth and marriage rates have been rising slowly since 1976, and the rate of increase in divorce has slowed since 1975.[46] But it is too soon to draw any conclusions from these figures.

THE GENERAL AND THE PARTICULAR

Overall, the trends in marriage, divorce, and childbearing since World War II appear to have been the result of a general, long-term historical process, on the one hand, and two specific historical events, on the other hand. The long-term process is the development of advanced industrial societies, one characteristic of which has been an increase over time in the proportion of married women who work outside the home. In the years since World War II, this trend accelerated in the United States and many other industrialized nations because of shifts in the demand for labor, rising real wages, greater educational attainment, better control over childbearing and, very recently, changes in attitudes about the employment of married women.[47] The great increase in female employment has altered, perhaps permanently, men's and women's roles in the family. Employment has made many married women less dependent on their husbands for support, and this development, in turn, may have increased the likelihood that unhappy couples will resort to divorce. Greater employment opportunities may have induced many single women to wait longer before marrying. At the same time improved contraception—another postwar development—may have influenced the trends by allowing couples to control the timing of childbearing, thus reducing unwanted births and helping women organize their work lives. Together, these society-wide changes in women's work lives and reproductive lives have promoted the acceleration of the long-term rise in divorce and the long-term fall in fertility that has characterized the United States since the mid-nineteenth century.

The specific historical events that interrupted these long-term patterns were the Great Depression and World War II. The disruption of family life and childbearing in the 1930s and the war years seems to have brought about, paradoxically, greater stability of family life and an increase in childbearing in the 1950s. This occurred, in part, through the social-psychological mechanism of instilling in the men and women born in the 1920s and 1930s a greater sense of the value of family life and child-rearing and by allowing only a modest standard of material comfort. A satisfying family life became more of a scarce resource during the depression and the war, and like most scarce resources, its value increased correspondingly. In addition, the depression influenced the trends of the 1950s through the demographic mechanism of reducing the size of the cohorts of the 1920s and 1930s. As a result of their small numbers, they were better able to take advantage of the opportunities offered by the postwar economic prosperity, and they were more likely to have the resources necessary to start or to enlarge their families.

Whether the legacy of the depression and the war will continue to influence marriage, divorce, and childbearing is the topic of much current debate. Some believe that the depression has set in motion long swings in fertility, marriage, and divorce that will continue indefinitely; others believe that the reversals of the 1950s were a one-time-only phenomenon. Until the data for the 1980s is known, one can only speculate. My opinion is that the swings produced by relative cohort size will be visible in the near future, but in sharply reduced magnitudes. I find it plausible that the values of people who grew up during the hard times of the 1930s were determined in large part by their childhood and adolescent experiences. Consequently, Easterlin can argue that some of the young couples in the 1950s brought to their marriages a modest standard of living that was unlikely to change, and Elder can argue that some also brought a strong preference for marriage and childrearing. Yet it does not follow, I believe, that growing up in the 1950s or the 1970s will determine adult preferences to the same extent. The young couples who will be marrying in the 1980s and 1990s did not face as children the kind of momentous, life-altering crisis that the depression was for many who grew up then. Despite their decreasing cohort size, they should be more likely as adults to modify their preferences for material goods, children, employment, and so forth as current circumstances change. And circumstances seem to me to be changing in such a way as to encourage the continued entry of women into the labor force—witness the recent, sharp changes in sex-role attitudes displayed in Figure 2-4—and continued low fertility. Thus I suspect that the cycles predicted by Easterlin will be similar to the damped oscillations of a child's swing—unless there is a further push from another depression or another world war, the swings will become progressively smaller and eventually fade altogether.

The process of change in postwar family life may be similar to the process of change in family life during the early years of industrialization. In his study of mid-nineteenth-century Hamilton, an industrializing city in what is now Ontario, Michael B. Katz found evidence that between 1851 and 1871 teenage youths became more dependent on their parents and that the foundation was laid for the stage of prolonged dependency we now call adolescence. In this and other ways, he argued, family ties and commitments grew stronger over time. Katz ascribed these changes to industrialization, in general, and to the depression of the late 1850s, in particular: "Any adequate explanation of this developmental process," he wrote of these changes, "must combine the interaction of long-term processes, such as modernization, with short-term crises, like depressions, which may accelerate or retard their pace. Only a theory which accommodates both the general and the particular can encompass adequately the kind of data presented here."[48] The same might be said of the explanations of the trends in marriage, divorce, and childbearing since World War II.

The postwar trends and the explanations for them would be of purely intellectual interest if they had no effect on the way we live. But in fact the trends have had important consequences for our lives and for our society.

3
The Consequences

What does it mean for people's lives and for the institution of the family when one out of two recent marriages is projected to end in divorce, when one out of six young women is likely to be still unmarried at age thirty, when a growing number of couples live together without marrying, when about one-third of all young adults can expect to find themselves eventually in a remarriage following a divorce?[1] In this chapter I examine the significance of these trends for the lives of individual adults and children and for the family patterns of American society. First, I look at the ways in which the trends in marriage, divorce, and remarriage have affected patterns of family life in our society as a whole. I examine the changes in the typical life course of Americans, in the composition of households and families, and in the role of marriage. Second, on the level of individuals, I consider the impact of the sharpest changes in family patterns —the greater levels of divorce and remarriage—on the everyday lives of adults and children.

MARRIAGE, DIVORCE, REMARRIAGE, AND THE LIFE COURSE

I have constructed lifetime marriage and divorce histories for three birth cohorts of women: those born in 1910 to 1914, 1930 to 1934, and 1950 to 1954. These three cohorts are roughly representative of three successive generations of Americans—those born early in the century, their children born around the time of the depression, and their grandchildren born during the postwar baby boom. The information for the two older cohorts was obtained from a 1975 Bureau of the Census survey in which approximately 100,000 adults were asked how many times they had ever married or divorced and the date of each marriage or divorce. For persons in the youngest of these three cohorts, who have not yet reached the midpoint of their lives, our information is, of course, less complete. Nevertheless, it is possible to project approximate lifetime levels of marriage, divorce, and remarrige for those born in the early postwar years, based on their experiences through the late 1970s and on the current age-specific rates of marriage and divorce. I have assembled and calculated projections for women born in 1950 to 1954 from estimates by Maurice J. Moore and Carolyn C. Rogers, the National Center for Health Statistics, and other sources.[2] These projections for the 1950 to 1954 cohort should not be taken as definitive; it is too soon to make precise predictions of the percentages ever divorcing or remarrying. But the estimates are useful in providing us with a picture of the likely experiences of these women and in allowing us to contrast the marital histories of the baby boom children with those of previous generations.

The lifetime experiences of these cohorts are displayed in Figure 3-1, which shows the cumulative percentage experiencing each of four events: a first marriage, a divorce, a remarriage after a divorce, and a second divorce. It shows, first of all, that almost everyone has married—96 percent of the 1930 to 1934 cohort and 94 percent of the oldest and youngest cohorts. Although these percentages are similar, there are sharp differences in the percentages who ever get divorced: only 15 percent of the women born in 1910 to 1914 have been divorced, but this rises to an estimated 25 percent for the women born during the depression and to an estimated 45 percent for the baby boom women. The differences continue in the percentages that ever remarry following a divorce: 12 percent for the 1910 to 1914 cohort, an estimated 20 percent for the 1930 to 1934 cohort, and an estimated 34 percent for the 1950 to 1954 cohort. The percentages ever divorcing a second time are small for the earlier cohorts: 1 percent for the 1910 to 1914 women and an estimated 5 percent for the 1930 to 1934 cohort; it is too soon to say what the percentage will be for the 1950 to 1954 cohort.

Figure 3-1 demonstrates the extent to which divorce and remarriage have changed from relatively rare experiences to much more common experiences during the twentieth century. If the experiences of the 1910 to 1914 cohort are representative of women born early in the century, then fewer than two in ten of the elderly women now alive were ever divorced, and only about one out of ten ever entered a second marriage after ending their first one in divorce. But for the young adult women of the 1970s, according to the estimates for women born in 1950 to 1954, divorce is likely to be a part of the lives of more than four out of ten, and about one in three may remarry following a divorce. For the generation in between—those who were born around the time of the depression and who reached adulthood following the war—the lifetime levels of divorce and remarriage also are in between: about one in four women will have

Figure 3-1 Percentage ever marrying, divorcing, and remarrying for three birth cohorts of women, 1910 to 1954. (Sources: see Appendix 4)

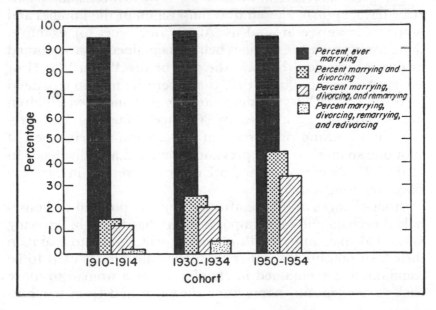

divorced and about two in ten will have remarried, according to the estimates for the 1930 to 1934 cohort.

The typical ages at divorce and at remarriage also declined slightly between the 1910 to 1914 cohort and the 1930 to 1934 cohort. The decline probably will continue with the 1950 to 1954 cohort, but it is too soon to precisely predict the medians for these women. Nevertheless, it is reasonable to expect that the 1950 to 1954 cohort will be a year or two younger when half of their divorces and remarriages have occurred than were the 1910 to 1914 cohort.[3] These changes in timing have been less impressive, however, than the changes in the volume of divorces and remarriages from one generation to the next. During the twentieth century, and especially during the postwar years, the most notable change in patterns of marital formation and dissolution is that divorce and remarriage increasingly have become a normal event in the course of a person's life.

HOUSEHOLD, FAMILY, AND MARRIAGE: PERSISTENCE AND CHANGE

The great increases in lifetime levels of divorce and remarriage have, in turn, altered the composition of the families and households we see around us. At any one time, for example, there are many more families being maintained by a separated or divorced person than was the case before World War II or even just a decade ago. In 1979 there were 3.8 million separated or divorced mothers heading families that included children under eighteen, an increase of 86 percent since 1970.[4] Moreover, in a growing proportion of all husband-wife families, at least one spouse has been previously married and divorced. In 1975, 5.2 million women and 5.7 million men were in a remarriage following a divorce.[5]

Other changes also have affected the composition of households. Perhaps the most important one has been the growing likelihood that unmarried individuals will choose to maintain their own households rather than live with kin. It used to be common, as I mentioned in chapter 1, for a woman to move back to her parents' home after she separated from her husband, but today separated and divorced women are much more likely to set up their own households. Never-married young adults, whose numbers have been increasing, are less likely to remain at home until they marry than they were twenty years ago. Similarly, more older, widowed people are living by themselves rather than moving in with their children.[6] It may be that the preferences of unmarried adults concerning living arrangements have changed. I suspect, however, that most unmarried adults always have preferred to live independently, only today they are more likely to have the financial resources to do so. In any case, the growth of households that do not contain a married couple has far outstripped the growth of husband-wife households. George Masnick and Mary Jo Bane project that between 1975 and 1990, 20 million additional households will be added to the current total, and four out of five will be maintained by unmarried persons, including 3 million single parents and 13.8 million single or previously married persons living outside of families. In contrast, Masnick and Bane project just an additional 400,000 households containing a married couple with children and 3 million more husband-wife households without children.[7]

As eye opening as these statistics on households are, they do have some limitations as indicators of trends in family life. As Masnick and Bane note, people move from one household to another more frequently than in the past; most of the young, single adults now maintaining households, for instance, eventually will marry—and many will divorce and then marry again. The statistics on household composition give us a snapshot of the living arrangements of Americans, and this picture is valuable to policymakers and to providers of goods and services. Yet families are increasingly extending across the boundaries of households, so that statistics about households are becoming less useful as a guide to the situation of families. Many separated, divorced, and remarried parents, for example, retain close ties to children living elsewhere, and many low-income single parents have strong family networks that extend across several households. (I discuss the changing relationship between household and family in more detail later in this chapter.)

Nevertheless, these statistics do show us that a smaller proportion of families and households contain a husband and wife than was the case ten or twenty years ago. And the proportion of husband-wife families in which one or both partners is remarried following a divorce has increased. Families headed by a couple in their first marriage, of course, have long been the dominant family form—both numerically and normatively—in American life. But the recent changes imply that although they are still numerically dominant (albeit less so), they must share their dominant position with two other increasingly common family forms: the single-parent family and the family of remarriage. If the estimates presented in Figure 3-1 prove at all accurate, one can no longer speak of families formed by divorce and by remarriage as unusual. Indeed, barring unforeseen reversals in the trends, a majority of all the children alive today will probably witness either the disruption of their parents' marriage or their own marriage by divorce. At any one time, then, the composition of families is more diverse than was the case in the 1950s.

Still, family life continues to center around marriage for most Americans. Most people marry, as we have seen, and most divorced people remarry within several years after their divorce. As others have argued, the increases in age at marriage and in divorce don't mean that marriage is on the way out or that family ties are fading.[8] During every period of rapid increases in divorce in the United States, concerned individuals have warned of the coming demise of the family; such alarmist sentiments have always been unfounded, and the warnings expressed in the 1960s and 1970s were no exception. By the beginning of the 1980s most commentators had decided that the latest reports of the imminent death of the family had been greatly exaggerated.

Having acknowledged the persistence and continuity of family life, however, we must also acknowledge that much has changed. Life in a single-parent family or a family formed by a remarriage has its unique and sometimes problematic aspects. Moreover, many more people must manage the difficult transition from being married to being divorced—a transition that seems to be no less painful merely because it is more common. And many more people must blend themselves, their children, their new spouses, and their new spouses' children into families formed by remarriages, which can prove to be a more complex and difficult task than one might expect.

Even the relationships of couples in first marriages have been altered by such developments as the changing roles of women, declining fertility, and more frequent recourse to divorce. In the 1950s Talcott Parsons argued that although some of its traditional functions were declining, the nuclear family centered on marriage was coming to specialize in two remaining functions: providing emotional support to adults and socializing young children.[9] Yet the post-1960 changes may have allowed more people to fulfill even these needs outside of marriage. Judith Blake, for instance, maintains that with more people living out of wedlock, having children out of wedlock, and voluntarily ending the state of wedlock, the line between being married and being unmarried has become increasingly blurred.[10] I think Blake may have overstated the lack of a distinctive role for marriage—as I argued in chapter 1, cohabitation seems to be less an alternative to marriage than a precursor—but it seems to be true that the functions of marriage increasingly can be fulfilled in other ways.

Thus many of the traditional reasons why people got married and stayed married are less compelling today. The greater economic independence of women means that marriage is less necessary as an economic partnership, as a common enterprise that creates a joint product neither partner could produce alone. And as the success of the economic enterprise becomes less crucial to husbands and wives, their personal satisfaction with their marriage becomes relatively more important. Consequently, it seems to me, husbands and wives are more likely today than in the past to evaluate their marriage primarily according to how well it satisfies their individual emotional needs. If their evaluation on these terms is unfavorable, they are likely to turn to divorce and then, perhaps, to another marriage.

On a societal level, then, patterns of marriage and family life are very different from what they were just a few decades ago. And the statistics I have presented suggest that among the most significant differences are the increasing levels of divorce and remarriage and the associated rise in the number of single-parent families and families formed by remarriage. When we shift our view from a societal level to the level of individuals, we find, not surprisingly, that the daily lives of adults and children in these postdivorce families differ in important ways from the typical experiences of people in families of first marriages. Let us take a closer look at how the rising levels of divorce and remarriage have affected the lives of individual adults and children in the United States.

FAMILY LIFE AFTER DIVORCE AND REMARRIAGE

The Aftermath of Divorce. Although social scientists have long been concerned about divorce, they produced little empirical research about its consequences until recently. Spurred by the latest rise in divorce, however, social scientists finally have begun to establish a body of knowledge about its effects on adults and children. This line of research is still new, and its findings are still tentative. On the one hand, the recent studies lend some support to the view that divorce can be beneficial in the long run for many of those involved. Some researchers, for instance, have produced findings in support of the oft-stated claim that children function better in a single-parent family than in a conflict-ridden nuclear family.[11] But on the other hand the studies also show that divorce is a traumatic process that can cause serious short-term psychological distress. And there are hints that for some people, the harmful effects may be longer lasting.

One reason why the newer studies emphasize the trauma of divorce more than some older writings on the subject is that much of the new research is based on intensive studies of recently separated adults and their children, and the period immediately following the separation is likely to be the most stressful. Robert S. Weiss studied adults who came to a series of eight-week discussion and counseling sessions he organized in Boston for persons separated less than one year. He found that the participants had ambivalent feelings toward their spouses even if they were relieved to have ended an unhappy marriage. Most reported a persistent feeling of attachment to their spouse, a sense of bonding that continued for several months whether the participant had initiated the separation or not. Thus many of the separated adults who attended Weiss's seminars felt an intermittent longing for their husbands or wives and an accompanying anxiety that Weiss labeled "separation distress." Only after the first year of separation did this attachment fade.[12]

Research by E. Mavis Hetherington and her colleagues indicates that the household routine is often disorganized during the first year after divorce. Hetherington followed for two years a group of middle-class families who had recently divorced and a comparison group of two-parent families. All of the families initially had preschool-aged children. She reported the predominance of a "chaotic lifestyle," as one divorced man called it, which seemed to persist throughout the first year after separation and then improve in the second year. Adults and children in the separated families were more likely to eat pickup meals at irregular times, the children's bedtimes were erratic, the children were more likely to arrive at school late, and so forth.[13]

Together, the Weiss and Hetherington studies caution that the first year after divorce or separation is often a time when the separated spouses experience ambivalence about the separation, increased anxiety, occasional depression, and personal disorganization—even if they were the ones who chose to end their unhappy marriages. Within a year, it appears, most separated adults have begun the process of reorganizing their lives, but it may take a few years more to firmly establish a stable identity and a new life situation.[14]

As for children, recent research demonstrates that they, too, experience an initial period of intense emotional upset after their parents separate. Judith S. Wallerstein and Joan B. Kelly studied 131 children from 60 recently separated families who sought the services of a counseling center in Marin County, California. They met with the children at the time of the divorce action, eighteen months later, and five years later. Theirs is the only study to follow a group of children for as long as five years after a parental divorce. At first, according to their study, almost all the children were profoundly upset. Their reactions varied according to age. Preschool children tended to be frightened and bewildered by the separation and to blame themselves for what had occurred; somewhat older children often expressed great anger. Adolescents were better able to comprehend the reasons for the divorce, but they often were deeply worried about the effects of the separation on their own future.[15] Moreover, research by Hetherington and others suggests that the adjustment to divorce may be more difficult for boys than for girls, although the reasons for this possible difference are not yet clear.[16]

Less is known about children's long-term adjustment to divorce. Hetherington found marked improvement in the relations between many of the parents and their preschool children between the first and second year after the divorce. One-half of the mothers and one-fourth of the fathers reported that two years after the divorce their relationships with their children had improved over the tension-filled days of their marriages.[17] Wallerstein and Kelly, however, presented a more pessimistic picture. Five years after their initial interview with the children, one-third were doing well psychologically, one-third were in the middle range of mental health, and one-third were still intensely unhappy and dissatisfied. In addition, at the five-year mark one-fourth of the children complained of loneliness—even in some cases where the custodial parent had remarried.[18]

The Hetherington study and the Wallerstein and Kelly study are far superior to past research on the effects of divorce on children, yet it is difficult to decide how representative these reports are. Both groups studied mostly middle-class and upper-middle-class families in large metropolitan areas, and Wallerstein and Kelly's subjects hailed from Marin County, which has gained national notoriety in recent years as almost a caricature of upper-middle-class marital instability. The Wallerstein and Kelly study also has other limitations. Because the investigators didn't compare the children with a control group of children in families that were not disrupted, it is difficult to judge how many of the problems exhibited by their subjects are common to all children—whether or not their parents have divorced. What's more, the families were a self-selected group who came to them seeking help. Families who seek counseling might represent the most distressed segment of the divorcing population.

Many of the Marin families had more than one child, and we might expect that if one child in the family was doing poorly, then the sibling also would be more likely to be troubled.

The only nationally representative information on the effects of divorce on children comes from a national survey of children aged seven to eleven and their parents conducted by Nicholas Zill for the Foundation for Child Development in 1976. Six percent of the children living with both original parents were described by their parents as needing professional help for an emotional, behavioral, mental, or learning problem; 5.5 percent actually had seen a psychologist or psychiatrist at some time. In contrast, 14 percent of the children in divorced households were seen as needing help, and 13 percent had actually seen a psychologist or psychiatrist.[19] These percentages, as Zill noted, can be interpreted in two ways. On the one hand, children of divorce were twice as likely to need assistance as were children from intact marriages, which suggests that children of divorce are at a greater risk of psychological distress. But on the other hand, six out of seven children of divorce were not seen as needing assistance, which suggests that most such children are able to cope adequately with the psychological consequences of their situation.

Zill's study refers only to children aged seven to eleven and did not follow parents and children over time. His brief, structured interviews could not yield the kind of in-depth information provided by the repeated testing and observation of Hetherington and of Wallerstein and Kelly on much smaller samples. Consequently, even with the results of this national survey in hand, there are still no firm estimates of the proportion of children who experience harmful psychological effects from parental divorce. But taking into account the little that is known from recent studies, we might conclude that: (1) almost all children experience an initial period of great emotional upset following a parental separation; (2) most return to normal development within one or two years following the separation; and (3) a minority of children experience some long-term psychological problems as a result of the separation.

Not all divorces, however, have the same consequences for children. This statement might seem obvious, but it was not obvious to researchers or clinicians until recently. The study of what helps or hinders children's adjustment to parental divorce is so new—few valuable studies were published before 1970— that we can draw only a few tentative conclusions. The first of these is that children seem to do better when they have a continuing relationship with both parents after the separation. Both the Wallerstein and Kelly and the Hetherington studies produced evidence that regular visits by the noncustodial parent— who is usually the father—helped the child greatly. Second, children do better when their parents can avoid involving them in their disputes. Parents who urge their children to take sides in the battle between the mother and father often increase the child's difficulties.[20] Third, children—particularly the younger ones—do better when the custodial parent can reestablish an orderly and supportive household routine. When the custodial parent can keep the house in order, get the children to school and to bed on time, maintain disciplinary standards, and provide emotional strength, the children can draw support from the parent and from the structure of their daily routine. When the parent is anxiety-ridden and depressed and the household is disorganized, as is common during the first year of separation, the children lose another pillar of support. The custodial parent, then, can help children by making a strong effort to function effectively as a parent.

Single Parents. It is often difficult for single parents to function effectively. Saddled with sole or primary responsibility for supporting themselves and their children, single parents frequently have too little time and too few resources to manage effectively. Robert Weiss, after several years of observing single parents, identified three common sources of strain. One is responsibility overload: single parents must make all the decisions and provide for all the needs of their families, a responsibility that at times can be overwhelming. Another is task overload: many single parents simply have too much to do, with working, housekeeping, and parenting; consequently, there is no slack time to meet unexpected demands. A third is emotional overload: single parents are always on call to give emotional support to their children, whether or not their own emotional resources are temporarily depleted.[21]

Earlier in the century a number of social scientists published studies purporting to show that the lack of a male presence in families maintained by single mothers was detrimental to children's development. "Fatherless families" were said to be unable to establish discipline over the children and to provide for proper sex-role identification. Proponents of this view tended to blame the absence of fathers for a variety of alleged pathologies among children from single-parent homes: juvenile delinquency, poorer academic achievement, less self-control, greater difficulty in adopting appropriate sex roles, and so forth. By the early 1970s, however, the contradictory results of a large number of studies had made it unclear that absence of the father was directly responsible for any of the supposed deficiencies of broken homes. In a comprehensive review article published in 1973, Elizabeth Herzog and Cecilia E. Sudia argued that the accumulated evidence failed to support any blanket generalizations about the effects of father absence. They claimed that previous researchers often erred in assuming that boys who lived with their separated or divorced mothers had no contact with their fathers or with other males. In addition, even when fathers were out of touch with their children, the behavior of the children could not be ascribed to the simple fact of father absence. More important than the presence or absence of the father, they concluded, is the ability of the custodial parent to manage her life and her children adequately. "The number of parents in the home," they wrote, "is likely to be less crucial than the family functioning of the present member—which is harder to assess."[22]

In fact, it seems likely that the most detrimental aspect of the absence of fathers from one-parent families headed by women is not the lack of a male presence but the lack of a male income. Divorced and separated women who are raising children often find that their economic position has deteriorated sharply. Thomas J. Espenshade recently reviewed the evidence on the economic consequences of divorce and concluded that "in general, wives are left worse off than their former husbands."[23] Many divorced women who were not employed in the years preceding their separation have difficulty reentering the job market. Others have worked at low-paying jobs that cannot provide the sole support for a family. When children are involved

—as they are in more than half of all divorces—they usually live with their mothers. In theory, divorced fathers should continue to help support their children, but in practice only a minority do so. In a 1979 Bureau of the Census survey, only 43 percent of all divorced and separated women with children present reported receiving child support payments, and the average annual payment was about $1,900. In the Panel Study of Income Dynamics, a national study of families who were interviewed and reinterviewed annually beginning in 1968, less than half of the women who married in 1968 and who divorced or separated by 1973 were receiving alimony or child support in 1973, with an average payment of $2,351 (in 1973 dollars) for whites and $1,554 for blacks. In a 1975 national survey of women only 44 percent of separated and divorced mothers reported that they had been awarded child support payments, and less than half of these reported receiving their support payments regularly.[24]

The results of the Panel Study of Income Dynamics demonstrated the consequences of these economic difficulties. Between 1968 and 1973, couples in the study who remained married saw their real family income increase by 21 percent. Men who were married in 1968 but who subsequently separated or divorced saw their family income decline by 19 percent. But when we take into account the smaller size of families headed by divorced men, many of whom live alone, and adjust their income for their reduced needs, their adjusted income actually rose by 17 percent. The income of women who separated or divorced by 1973 decreased 29 percent, and even after adjusting for needs, their incomes showed a 7 percent drop. Thus, after divorce, men were doing better, relative to their changed needs, than when they were married. Women, on the other hand, were doing worse.[25]

Despite economic pressures, life in a single-parent family also has its rewards, foremost the relief from marital conflict. In addition, single parents may gain increased self-esteem from their ability to manage the demands of work life and family life by themselves. They may enjoy their independence and their close relationships to their children.[26] Some writers argue that women are particularly likely to develop an increased sense of self-worth from the independence and greater control over their life they achieve after divorce.[27]

Still, single parents must overcome the considerable difficulties caused by lack of support. To be sure, many single parents, particularly those with low incomes, receive support from a network of kin, but the resources of these networks usually are limited and spread thin. (I discuss kin networks in the next chapter.) The withdrawal of the father's economic contribution often forces the mother to assume the entire financial burden, and this economic pressure, in turn, means that she has less time for child care and for her personal life. If some female-headed households fail to provide the attention and care children need, the failure may result more from the harried life of the overburdened single mother than from the absence of a man in the home.

Because most divorced mothers establish a separate household and keep their children with them, single parents are much more visible today. Their greater visibility and greater numbers have stimulated a demand for public assistance. Some observers have called for the creation of maintenance allowances for single parents, modeled after programs in some Western European countries.[28] Currently the only forms of income maintenance available to single mothers are Aid to Families with Dependent Children and food stamps, which provide a modest level of support for low-income families.

Single parents, along with the increasing number of parents in two-earner, two-parent families, form a growing constituency in favor of expanded support for child care. If the rate of divorce and the proportion of married women in the labor force continue to rise, then this constituency will continue to grow in the 1980s. At the present time, there is limited federal support for child care, mostly in the form of a tax credit that working parents can claim.[29] Single parents with preschool-aged children are particularly constrained by the difficulty of obtaining satisfactory care. In the June 1977 Current Population Survey, one-third of all nonemployed, divorced and widowed mothers with children under age five said they would be looking for work if satisfactory child care were available; nearly half of those working part time said they would work more hours if they could find satisfactory care.[30] The term "satisfactory care" was not defined in the survey, so it is difficult to know exactly what the respondents had in mind. Yet their replies suggest that the unavailability of satisfactory child care may prevent many single mothers from improving their economic lot.

Remarriage. For most divorced men and women, living as a single adult is a temporary phase. As I noted in chapter 1, most divorced persons remarry—about three-fourths of all women and an even larger proportion of all men. Moreover, about half of all the divorced persons who will remarry do so within three years after their divorce. In the United States and other western societies, remarriage has been the traditional answer to many of the problems faced by single parents. In the Plymouth Colony, for example, it was not unusual for one parent to die before the children reached adulthood. Most of the widows and widowers remarried within a short time, according to a study by John Demos, often within one year. The surviving parent, Demos emphasized, remarried quickly not out of any lack of respect for the decreased spouse but rather because it took two parents to meet the demands of raising a family in the harsh environment of the colony.[31] Today, despite the changes in American society, many divorced parents remarry because they need assistance in similar ways. Remarriage improves the financial situation of a divorced mother and provides another adult to share the household tasks and responsibilities. In addition, remarrying is a way to end the loneliness and isolation many divorced persons experience.

Whereas divorce often weakens the ties between children and their relatives on the side of the noncustodial parent (usually the father), remarriage creates a new set of relationships with a stepparent and his or her kin. When at least one spouse has children from a previous marriage, the family of remarriage can extend far beyond the bounds of the family of first marriage. Stepparents, stepchildren, stepsiblings, stepgrandparents, the new spouses of noncustodial parents, and other kin all may play a role in family life. This expanded set of family relationships in a remarriage can help compensate children for the loss of kin they may suffer after their parents divorce. Children whose custodial parent remarries often seem to inherit not only a stepparent but also a set of stepgrandparents and other step-kin. And since many children retain some contact with their noncustodial parent and grandparents, some children whose parents remarry may have contact with more kin than they did before their father and mother separated. The quality and quantity of time children spend with kin and step-kin after a remarriage is a subject on which research is just beginning.[32]

In postdivorce families, the children from previous marriages create links between households because of their visits with the noncustodial parent—visits that frequently require communication among the divorced parents, the new stepparent, and the noncustodial parent's new spouse. These increasingly common links across households are forcing us to alter the way we define family and kinship. To illustrate, let us consider the case in which a married couple with two children divorces and the wife retains custody of the children, as shown in panel A of Figure 3-2. If we ask the divorced mother who is in her immediate family, she certainly would include her children, but she might well exclude her ex-husband, who now lives elsewhere. If we ask her children who is in their immediate family, however, we might get a different answer. If the children still see their father regularly, as is often the case, they probably would include both their father and their mother as part of their family.[33] And if we ask the ex-husband who is in his immediate family, he might include his children, whom he continues to see, but not his ex-wife. Thus after divorce, mother, father, and children all may have a different conception of who is in their immediate family. In fact, one can no longer define "the family" or "the immediate family" except in relation to a particular person.

The situation becomes more complicated in a remarriage that involves children from previous marriages. Let us suppose that the mother remarries someone who also has children from a previous marriage and that the mother then has additional children with her new spouse, as diagramed in panel B of Figure 3-2. Now the mother's household contains persons in four different positions—the mother herself, the father/stepfather, the children from her first marriage, and the children from her remarriage. The persons in each of these four positions may have

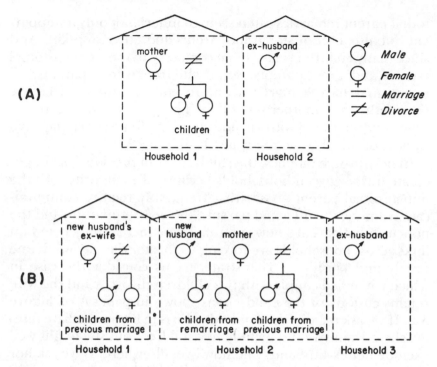

Figure 3-2 Kinship relations and household structure after divorce (A) and after the mother's remarriage (B).

a different conception of who is in their family. The children from the remarriage are likely to include all the members of their household and no one else. The mother's new husband may well include three sets of children: those from his previous marriage, his new marriage, and from his wife's previous marriage. Not all remarriages involve family structures this complex, of course, but whenever children are present from previous marriages, multiple definitions arise.

In these kinds of postdivorce families, there is no invariant definition of the immediate family that we can apply to all parties. Instead, a household formed by a divorce or remarriage that involves children from a previous marriage becomes the intersection of an overlapping set of relationships, each of which constitutes an immediate family for one or more members of the household. There are no fixed rules as to who should be included as members of each of these families. The noncustodial parent, for example, may or may not be thought of by his children as a member of their family, depending on whether he retains his ties to them. Although each person in a postdivorce household may have a clear idea of who belongs to his or her immediate family, the definitions of the immediate family are likely to vary widely among persons in the same structural positions in different households.

It also is unclear exactly who a person's more distant relatives are. In many households linked by the ties of broken marriages, there is considerable interaction among people whose only relationship is through the broken marriage. Anthropologist Paul Bohannan has labeled these linked households "divorce chains" and the persons related through the ties of broken marriages "quasi-kin."[34] For example, in panel B of Figure 3-2, the children from the mother's previous marriage might play with the children from her new husband's previous marriage when the husband's children come to visit. Over time, these two sets of children might begin to consider themselves relatives, although they have no formal ties to each other.

Common Problems in Remarriages. The ambiguity about the definition of kinship in families of divorce and remarriage is mirrored in the confusion over how to resolve some of the practical problems these families experience. Our society, oriented toward first marriages, provides little guidance to currently divorced adults, to remarried adults, and to their children as to how they should manage their unfamiliar and complex family lives. The lack of institutionalized—that is, generally accepted —ways of resolving problems is particularly noticeable for the families of remarriages following divorce.[35]

Many aspects of remarried life are similar to life in a first marriage and are subject to established rules of behavior. And remarriage itself is an institutionalized solution to the ambiguous status of the divorced parent. But for remarried adults and their children day-to-day life includes many problems for which there are no institutionalized solutions. These problems can range from deciding what a stepchild should call his or her stepparent, to resolving the sexual tensions that can emerge between step-relatives in the absence of a well-defined incest taboo, to defining the financial obligations of husbands to their spouses and children from current and previous marriages.[36] Bohannan, noting the lack of the relevant social norms, wrote in 1970, "The present situation approaches chaos, with each individual set of families having to work out its own destiny without any realistic guidelines."[37]

Stepparents, for example, are often unsure about how severely they can discipline their stepchildren. Some stepparents, determined not to show favoritism toward their own children, discipline them more harshly than their stepchildren. Others have difficulty establishing themselves as a disciplinarian with their stepchildren. These uncertainties seem to result from the sharing of the parental role by the stepparent and the noncustodial biological parent, who usually retains some ties to the child.[38] Years ago, when most remarriages took place after widowhood, this sharing of fatherhood or motherhood was very rare. Now, even though most remarriages follow a divorce, generally accepted guidelines for sharing parenthood still have not emerged.

Perhaps because of the lack of social support, families of remarriage are more likely to show indications of difficulties than one might expect, given that the parents are older and presumably more mature than when they entered into their first marriages. For example, although several studies have shown little difference between the adjustment of children living with two natural parents as opposed to those living with one natural parent and one stepparent, when differences have been found, it is the children in stepparent homes who have been less well adjusted.[39] In his 1976 national survey of children aged seven to eleven, Zill reported that children living with a mother and a stepfather were significantly more likely to have been described by the parent as needing help in the last year for an emotional, behavioral, mental, or learning problem than children living with two natural parents or with just their mothers alone.[40] Neil Kalter reported that girls living with a mother and a stepfather were overrepresented in a sample of outpatients at a midwestern clinic. Among girls aged twelve and over, those with stepfathers had significantly higher incidences of aggression toward parents and peers, sexual activity, drug involvement, and school-related problems than girls living with a father and a mother.[41] The evidence is still very tentative, but it suggest that children may undergo a difficult period of adjustment when a stepparent is introduced into the home. The adjustment may be particularly difficult in the case of a stepfather and stepdaughter—perhaps because of the sexual tensions arising from the lack of a clear incest taboo.[42]

Furthermore, as I mentioned in chapter 1, the divorce rate for remarried persons is modestly but consistently higher than for persons in first marriages. Some people believe that the rate is higher because the remarried population contains a higher proportion of people who, for one reason or another, are likely to resort to divorce if their marriage falters.[43] I believe, on the contrary, that many of the difficulties of families of remarriage, including the higher divorce rate and the higher incidence of some emotional problems among children, stem from the lack of institutionalized support. The absence of accepted guidelines means that these often complex families must resolve perplexing issues by themselves. As a result, I would argue, solving everyday problems is sometimes impossible without engendering conflict and confusion among family members.[44]

Divorce and Remarriage: Costs and Benefits. Because of the rise in divorce, more and more parents and children—currently more than one million families per year—are experiencing the distress of marital separation. Yet the process of divorce does benefit many adults who go through it, because it frees them from the tensions of an unhappy marriage. Most divorced persons say that their lives would have been worse had they not separated from their spouses.[45] At least one partner in every disrupted marriage chooses to divorce and, as best we can judge, the benefits of divorce to that partner outweigh the costs. I suspect, however, that few adults who are about to separate are prepared for the intense emotional, social, and economic difficulties that often occur during the first years after separation.

The situation of children whose parents divorce is more problematic. With few exceptions, children do not want their parents to separate. It is probably true that children are better off, as many researchers have claimed, living with one separated parent than living in a home torn apart by intense conflict between two parents. What if, however, the parents are unhappy with their marriage, have lost much of their affection for or interest in one another, but are able to limp along without much hostility or open conflict? No one knows how many couples in this situation decide to divorce, and no one can say whether the children in these families would be better off if their parents divorced. Moreover, Wallerstein and Kelly found that some parents in conflict-ridden marriages still were able to share in maintaining a loving and supportive relationship with their children. And even though many of the children in their study doubted that their parents were happily married, even though many were well aware of a long history of difficulties between their parents, very few greeted divorce with relief; rather, most were shocked and distressed at the news that their parents were separating.[46] It is not at all clear, then, that most children benefit from divorce.

It appears, nevertheless, that most children recover from their initial distress and resume normal development within a few years. At the five-year mark, if Wallerstein and Kelly's study is at all representative, only a minority are still experiencing problems related to the divorce. We know very little about the longer-range effects of parental divorce on children's later lives. Several statistical studies suggest that people whose parents divorced are somewhat more likely to end their own marriages in divorce.[47] Yet these studies, which are based on survey data, include only rough indicators of the past family history of the subject, and they don't make clear the reasons for this modest association. Perhaps the experience of witnessing the breakup of the parents' marriage does, somehow, increase the likelihood that the child also will divorce, but we need more sophisticated studies to say for sure.

It is possible, however, that children whose parents divorce may come to place a higher value on a stable marriage and home life. There is a striking parallel between Glen Elder's reports on the experiences of adolescents in deprived homes during the depression and more recent reports on the experiences of older children who live with a recently separated parent. As I pointed out in chapter 2, Elder noted the "downward extension of adult-like experience" as teenaged boys took part-time jobs and spent more time with their peers, while teenaged girls helped more around the home.[48] Similarly, Weiss found that older children often were an important source of assistance to their separated or divorced mothers: they took on additional household tasks, were consulted in more family decisions, and provided emotional support. Thus many of them were thrust into situations where they, like children in the depression, were required to behave more like adults.[49] Elder reported that when they reached adulthood, the children from deprived homes placed a higher value on marriage, home, and family than did those from nondeprived homes. They were part of a generation that married early, had children faster, and divorced less than one would expect from the historical trend. I think it is worth considering the possibility that the long-term effects of parental divorce on children may also have some benign or even positive effects on later family life, as appears to be the case with the long-term effects of growing up in the depression.

We should remember, in addition, that most divorced adults will spend most of the rest of their lives not living alone or in a single-parent family but in a family of remarriage. Most remarried adults are satisfied with their current marriages and believe them to be far superior to their failed first marriages.[50] Although parents and children in a family of remarriage can have difficulty adjusting to their complex and poorly institutionalized situation, remarriage improves the financial situation of single parents, creates an additional set of kin to supplement the remaining ties to the kin of noncustodial parents, and provides another stable source of affection and emotional support. The long-term adjustment of many adults and children to divorce may depend on the support provided by remarriage.

I think there is reason to believe that the degree of difficulty of adults and children in single-parent and stepparent families may be reduced in coming years. As I have mentioned, many of the problems of single and remarried parents can be traced to the lack of generally accepted guidelines for behavior in these kinds of families. Divorce and remarriage after divorce still are relatively new phenomena on a large scale in the United States.

As I showed in chapter 1, only one out of six women born in 1910 to 1914 divorced during their lifetimes, and as late as the 1920s more of the persons who were remarrying had been widowed than had been divorced. During the 1960s and early 1970s, the divorce rate increased with unprecedented speed, but since 1975 the rate of increase has slowed.[51] We may now have at least a brief respite from rapid change, a period in which adjustments can be made.

The sharp increases in divorce and remarriage since 1960 mean that many more Americans than ever before are grappling with the special problems of family life after divorce and after remarriage. With greater numbers, the amount of communication among these families has increased. In the past few years, several associations of divorced and remarried parents have been formed, and numerous newsletters, pamphlets, and books have appeared. I think it likely that these families will generate ways of resolving common problems which will come to be widely accepted as standards of conduct. For instance, I suspect that in the near future, stepparents will know more about how strict they should be with their stepchildren, and divorced parents will know more about what degree of assistance they can expect from their ex-spouses. The creation of a body of social norms will not eliminate the problems of these family members, but it may reduce the potential for confusion and conflict. If so, family life after divorce and remarriage may be somewhat easier to manage than it is today.

So far, I have discussed the changing patterns of marriage, divorce, and remarriage among Americans in general. But during the last few decades, the differences between the typical marital patterns of whites and blacks have become more pronounced, as the next chapter shows.

4

Black-White Differences

Throughout this book I have discussed trends in family patterns for the American population as a whole. As I mentioned in the Introduction, I could not, in such a short book, thoroughly examine the changing behavior of the many ethnic, regional, religious, and social class groupings that social scientists study. Moreover, there is reason to believe that the postwar trends up and down have been parallel for most groups. Ronald R. Rindfuss and James A. Sweet, for instance, carefully studied the trends in childbearing since World War II, expecting to find that some groups in the population had not followed the overall cycle of boom and bust. To their surprise, they found that virtually every group they looked at showed the same pattern— fertility peaked in the late 1950s and declined thereafter.[1] Other investigators have found evidence that some group differences may have decreased in the past few decades: the childbearing rates of Catholics and non-Catholics have converged, for example, and Catholic versus non-Catholic differences in the probability of separation and divorce appear to have decreased somewhat.[2] All of these findings suggest that it is useful and statistically acceptable to study trends for the entire population, and that is the strategy I have followed.

Yet one set of group differences deserves separate consideration: those between the typical family patterns of blacks and of whites. Some of these differences—in out-of-wedlock childbearing and in household structure, for instance—appear to have existed since slavery or at least since the latter half of the nineteenth century. Moreover, most of the various rates examined in previous chapters appear to have moved in the same direction for both groups since World War II. Black fertility rates, for example, peaked in the late 1950s just as white fertility rates did, and both black and white fertility rates subsequently declined. There was a short surge of divorce among blacks immediately after the war, just as for whites. And the annual divorce rate seems to have increased at about the same speed for both groups in the 1960s.[3] But in other important ways the family lives of blacks and whites appear to have diverged since World War II. Some of these divergent trends—such as the widening difference between the proportion of white and black families maintained by a woman—have become the subject of considerable attention and debate. Because of recent trends, the differences between the typical family lives of white and black Americans may be greater in the 1980s than they were in the 1950s.

THE DIVERGENT TRENDS

No trend illustrates this divergence more clearly than the changing timing of marriage. In the late nineteenth century—the earliest period for which we have reliable information—and throughout the first half of the twentieth century, blacks tended to marry at a younger age than did whites. Between 1940 and 1950, however, the average age at which whites married began to decrease, and by mid-century there was little difference between the two groups. Figure 4-1 displays the percentage of white and nonwhite women aged twenty to twenty-four who were single (that is, never married) in a given year.[4] Around the turn of the century the percentage single was much greater for white women, but by 1950 the difference had disappeared.

After 1950 the trends turned around. The percentage single dropped further for white women in the 1950s, as more of them married earlier. But for nonwhites the percentage single rose during the 1950s, and it rose at a faster rate in the 1960s

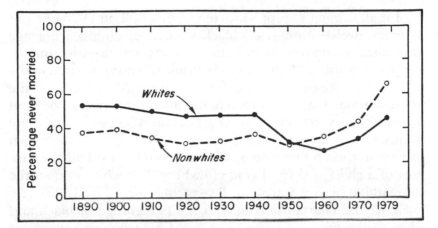

Figure 4-1 Percentage never married for women aged 20 to 24, by color, 1890–1979. (Sources: for 1890–1940, Paul Jacobson, *American Marriage and Divorce* [New York: Rinehart, 1959], p. 62; for 1950–1979, U.S. Bureau of the Census: *U.S. Census of Population: 1950*, vol. IV, Special Reports, pt. 2, chap. D, Tables 1 and 2; *U.S. Census of Population: 1960*, vol. I, Characteristics of the Population, pt. I: U.S. Summary, Table 1976; *U.S. Census of Population: 1970*, vol. I, Characteristics of the Population, pt. I: U.S. Summary, sec. 2, Table 203; Current Population Reports, series P-20, no. 349, "Marital Status and Living Arrangements: March 1979," Table 1.)

and at an even faster rate in the 1970s. In 1979, despite the movement toward later marriage among whites in the 1960s and 1970s, the percentage single among nonwhite women far exceeded the percentage single among white women—66 percent versus 46 percent for those aged twenty to twenty-four. Since World War II, then, a historic difference between blacks and whites in marriage timing has been turned on its head: blacks used to marry earlier than whites, but now they marry later.[5]

The later age at marriage for blacks also is associated with another difference between blacks and whites—the proportion of women who give birth to a child before they marry. Black women have had much higher annual rates of out-of-wedlock childbearing than white women since at least 1940, when adequate statistics first became available. Between 1940 and about 1960 the rate of out-of-wedlock childbearing rose sharply for both whites and blacks. After 1960, however, the rate continued to rise for whites but began to decline for black women aged twenty and over, and since about 1970 the rate has been declining for all women except white teenagers. Still, in 1978 one out of every twelve unmarried black women of childbearing age gave birth, compared to one out of every seventy-two unmarried white women.[6] In a national sample of young women in the late 1960s and early 1970s, for example, 20 percent of the never-married blacks eighteen to nineteen years old, 44 percent of those twenty to twenty-one years old, and 59 percent of those twenty-two to twenty-three years old had a child of their own present in their household or were responsible for half the support of a child of theirs living elsewhere. For white women the comparable figures were 2 to 3 percent.[7]

Figure 4-2 charts the trends in the percentage of black and white brides aged fourteen to twenty-four who were pregnant or had already given birth to a child at the time of their first marriage. Since the early 1960s the percentage of brides with a child has risen sharply among blacks and less dramatically among whites. Conversely, the percentage of pregnant brides

Figure 4-2 Childbearing status at time of first marriage, for women who were first married at 14 to 24 years, by period of first marriage, by race. (Source: U.S. Bureau of the Census, Current Population Reports, series P-20, no. 325, "Fertility of American Women: June 1977," Table 16.)

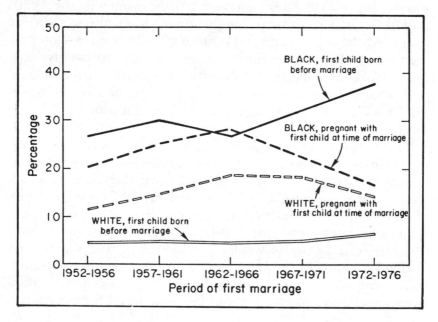

has dropped since the early 1960s for both groups, with the sharper drop occurring among blacks. One reason why proportionally fewer brides are pregnant now is the availability of better contraceptive techniques and of abortion. But the divergent trends in premarital pregnancies and premarital births for brides suggest another reason—that single women who become pregnant are less likely to marry before they give birth. Having a child out of wedlock appears to have become a much more acceptable option for pregnant, unmarried women.[8]

One might expect that after a single woman has a child, she would be less attractive to men looking for a wife, and her chances of marrying would be reduced. If so, then the large proportion of single mothers among blacks might further raise the average age at marriage. But whether a single black woman has a child seems to have little bearing on whether she marries subsequently, at least according to the behavior of a national sample of young women who were followed for several years during the late 1960s and early 1970s.[9] Having a first child and getting married appear to have become unrelated events for more and more black women during the postwar period. To be sure, the separation of marriage and first childbirth also has occurred to a more limited extent for whites in the postwar period, but it is far more pervasive among blacks. Because of this development and because of the rapid post-1960 decline in the rate of childbearing among married women, about two out of every three black women who gave birth to a first child in the late 1970s were unmarried, compared to about one out of eight white women.[10]

The divergence in the age at marriage for blacks and whites since 1950 also has contributed to an increasingly dissimilar distribution of black and white adults by current marital status. This increasing dissimilarity can be seen in Figure 4-3, which displays the current marital statuses of black and white women aged twenty-five to forty-four in 1950 and in 1979. People in this age range are old enough to have married and divorced, but young enough to be raising children and to probably not be widowed. The two pie charts for 1950 show a greater proportion of separated women and a smaller proportion of currently married women among nonwhites. As I noted in chapter 1,

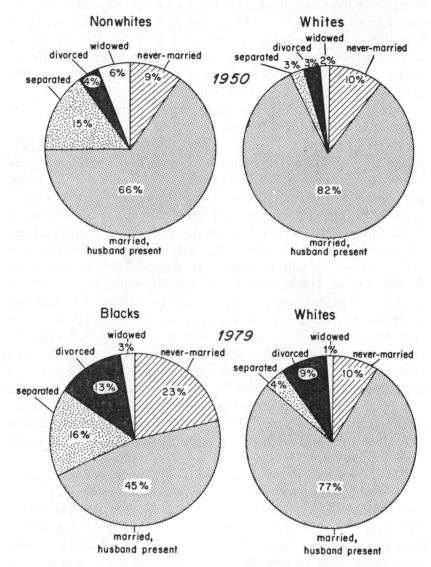

Figure 4-3 Current marital status of women aged 25 to 44, by race or color, 1950 and 1979. (Sources: U.S. Bureau of the Census. For 1979, Current Population Reports, series P-20, no. 349; for 1950, *U.S. Census of Population: 1950,* vol. IV, Special Reports, chap. D, p. 2.)

black married couples have a greater probability of separating than do white couples, and blacks who are separated tend to remain in this status longer before obtaining a divorce. Consequently, at any one time there are proportionally more blacks than whites who are separated but not divorced. In addition, once they have divorced, blacks tend to take longer to remarry, which means that proportionally more blacks also are divorced and not remarried at any time.[11]

By 1979 the black-white differences were even greater. The proportion of twenty-five- to forty-four-year-old women who were single more than doubled for blacks but hardly changed for whites during the twenty-nine intervening years. The separated and divorced categories expanded at about the same rate for both groups, and the proportion of twenty-five- to forty-four-year-old women in these two categories remained larger for blacks. Overall, the single, separated, and divorced categories all increased for blacks to the point that in 1979 less than half of all black women aged twenty-five to fourty-four reported that they were married with a husband present in the household, as opposed to about three-fourths of all white women aged twenty-five to forty-four.

The absence of a husband in the household, however, does not necessarily mean that there are no men in the family or that there is no contact between the woman and her partner or that a strong and stable family structure is lacking. Furthermore, as I mentioned in chapter 1, the category "separated" is plagued by an unknown amount of misreporting. Some of the so-called separated women may, in fact, have never married; others may not wish to disclose to a government interviewer that they are currently married.

Yet even taking into account these limitations, the census data arrayed in Figure 4-3 suggest that during the postwar period some aspects of the living arrangements and marital experiences of blacks and whites diverged sharply. For blacks, later marriage, a higher rate of separation and divorce, and more time spent in the separated and divorced statuses meant that relatively fewer people were currently married. To demonstrate the extent of this divergence more clearly, I have calculated indexes of dissimilarity between the current marital sta-

Table 4-1. Indexes of dissimilarity in current marital status between nonwhites and whites (for 1950 and 1960) and between blacks and whites (for 1970 and 1979) aged 25 to 44, by sex.

Year	Males	Females
1950	11.7	17.1
1960	16.4	20.9
1970	15.7	25.1
1979	20.5	32.0

Sources: U.S. Bureau of the Census. 1950: *U.S. Census of Population: 1950.* vol. IV, *Special Reports*, pt. 2, chap. D, "Marital Status," Tables 1 and 2. 1960: *U.S. Census of Population: 1960.* Subject Reports. "Persons by Family Characteristics," Final Report PC(2)-4B, Table 2. 1970: *U.S. Census of Population: 1970.* Subject Reports. "Persons by Family Characteristics," Final Report PC(2)-4B, Table 2. 1979: *Current Population Reports*, series P-20, no. 349, "Marital Status and Living Arrangements: March, 1979."

tuses of blacks and whites aged twenty-five to forty-four in 1950, 1960, 1970, and 1979, by sex. The index values represent the percentage of all whites (or all nonwhites or blacks) who would have to change their marital status in order for the two groups to have the same proportion in each status. The values are listed in Table 4-1, which shows that between 1950 and 1979 the indexes increased by nearly 90 percent for women and by about 75 percent for men. In 1950, about 12 percent of all white men would have had to change status in order for non-white and white men to have the same distribution; in 1979, 21 percent would have had to change. For women, the comparable index values were 17 and 32 percent.[12]

ACCOUNTING FOR THE DIFFERENCES

Why have some aspects of the typical family patterns of blacks and whites diverged in the past few decades? Recent scholarship has rejected some conventional explanations, but scholars have not as yet offered a satisfactory alternative. Forty years ago, E.

Franklin Frazier, a sociologist at the University of Chicago, proposed what has become the best-known explanation in his classic work, *The Negro Family in the United States*.[13] There are two parts to Frazier's argument. First, he attributed the high levels of marital instability and out-of-wedlock childbearing among blacks to the long-lasting effects of slavery on black family life. According to Frazier, the lack of formal marriage among slaves and the frequency with which fathers and children were sold away, never to see their kin again, shattered all the bonds of slave families except the link between mother and child. Because of this legacy of slavery, Frazier believed, black families after the Civil War continued to be centered around mothers and children, with out-of-wedlock childbearing and marital separation common.

The second part of Frazier's argument was that the newly freed blacks and their children's generation were "simple rural folk" whose way of life fit the traditional patterns of a rural, agricultural society. Out-of-wedlock childbearing and marital instability existed, but the well-established rural community, he argued, was able to support its members and control antisocial conduct. When these simple folk began to migrate in large numbers to the North, however, they encounted the unfamiliar way of life of the industrial city, with its formal, impersonal, instrumental relations. Cut off from the moral support of the friends and relatives they left behind, the migrants often found it difficult to adjust to the city, according to Frazier, and their lives often became disorganized. With no adequate means of maintaining social control, the neighborhoods full of black migrants suffered from high rates of crime, juvenile delinquency, and other assorted ills, while black family life deteriorated. Here Frazier's argument parallels the more general theories of urban growth and development propounded by his colleagues at Chicago, such as Ernest Burgess and Louis Wirth. They maintained that much of the "social disorganization" in the slums of Chicago resulted from the clash between the rational, impersonal way of life in a modern city and the traditional values of the millions of immigrants who were pouring into Chicago from Europe and the American South in the late nineteenth and early twentieth centuries.

Until recently, Frazier's argument was endorsed by most observers of black family life—Daniel P. Moynihan, for instance, cited Frazier approvingly in his controversial 1965 report, *The Negro Family: The Case for National Action*.[14] But now there is reason to believe that it is an unsatisfactory explanation of contemporary trends in black family life. For one thing, historians who have studied public and private records have found evidence that family and kinship ties were much stronger among slaves and antebellum free blacks than had been assumed and that two-parent families were more common than we had thought.

Historian Herbert G. Gutman has done the most extensive study, based on a detailed examination of plantation records, manuscript census schedules, and other documents spanning the period from 1750 to 1925. Gutman found evidence that most slaves formed stable unions and lived together until they died, unless one of them was sold away. Most slave children, he contends, grew up in two-parent families with strong ties to a larger kin group. Moreover, Gutman and others have found that a high proportion of black families in the late nineteenth and early twentieth centuries contained two parents. Gutman concluded:

> At all moments between 1880 and 1925—that is, from an adult generation born in slavery to an adult generation about to be devastated by the Great Depression of the 1930s and the modernization of Southern agriculture afterward—the typical Afro-American family was lower class in status and headed by two parents. This is so in the urban and rural South in 1880 and in 1900 and in New York City in 1925.[15]

Yet beginning sometime after 1925, the proportion of black families headed by two parents began to decline, and this decline became more pronounced in the 1960s and 1970s. According to Gutman, in 1925 five out of six black children under the age of six in New York City lived with both parents.[16] In the United States in 1979, however, only three out of seven black children under age six were living with both parents.[17] It seems, therefore, that single-parent black families began to occur on a much larger scale within the last fifty years. If so, then it is difficult to argue that this change in family structure was a lingering effect of a slavery system that had ended more than half a century before. And if two-parent families were more common under slavery than we had imagined, the legacy-of-slavery argument is further weakened. The work of revisionist scholars such as Gutman suggests that the legacy of slavery for black families was much less imposing than Frazier and others had assumed.

The recent research also casts doubt upon the hypothesis that contemporary trends in black family patterns reflect a culture clash between simple rural folk and complex urban societies. In Philadelphia in 1880, for example, Southern-born blacks— many of whom were slaves or the children of slaves—were less likely to be living in families headed by women then were Northern-born blacks.[18] The great surge of black migration to the North began after World War I, yet Gutman found a preponderance of two-parent families in New York as late as 1925. He reported, in fact, that in New York City in 1905 and again in 1925, six out of seven black households and subfamilies contained a husband or a father.[19] Findings such as these refute the idea that the family life of recent migrants deteriorated.

Still, the changes in the timing of marriage displayed in Figure 4-1 might partially reflect the influence of rural to urban migration. Since World War I, when the northward movement began, the percentage single among nonwhite women aged twenty to twenty-four has increased during every decade except the 1940s. Some of this increase may indicate the adjustment of blacks to the later marriage age typical of the urban North. Yet the movement to the North cannot account for all of the changes in marriage timing. In the early 1970s, for instance, the number of blacks moving from the North to the South exceeded by a small amount the number moving from the South to the North—thus reversing the historic pattern of northward migration.[20] But during the 1970s the percentage single among blacks increased faster than ever before. Many of the young black adults in the 1970s were second, third, or fourth generation northerners. At least in recent years, therefore, something other than a move from the farm to the city has caused the changing marriage patterns of blacks.

I think it is clear from the evidence reviewed that a substantial part of the current differences between black and white family patterns are of recent origin. The contemporary divergence goes back no further than the depression and has accelerated since 1960. To be sure, there have long been differences between the average black and white family in household structure, ties with kin, and out-of-wedlock childbearing. But some of the specific differences that have received the most attention, such as the proportion of families maintained by a woman, are much more noticeable now than in the past. In 1960, for example, 21 percent of black families were maintained by a woman, a proportion roughly comparable to figures reported by historians who have studied census records from the latter half of the nineteenth century. The comparable figure for white families in 1960 was 8 percent. Yet by 1979, 41 percent of black families were maintained by a woman, compared to 12 percent among white families.[21] Moreover, the lesson I draw from the debate over Frazier's thesis is that the causes of the recent divergence lie in the contemporary situation of urban, Northern blacks rather than in a lingering heritage of slavery or a clash of traditional and modern cultures. The family patterns of urban blacks differ today from the patterns among whites in large part because of differences in the current experiences of city-born-and-bred blacks and whites. Instead of looking back to slavery or to the rural, postbellum South, we need to look at life in the cities today.

Scholars are just beginning the task of determining what it is about the contemporary situation of blacks that has brought about this recent alteration of family patterns. One development that may help us understand the recent changes is the emergence of sharper social class distinctions between the growing middle-class segment of the black population and the lower-class segment. Middle-class blacks, according to some observers, have benefited from increased educational and employment opportunities in the last few decades, while the lot of the lower-class black has continued to deteriorate. Sociologist William Julius Wilson, for instance, maintains that since World War II many talented and well-educated blacks have been able to find stable, well-paying jobs in the corporate and government sectors of the economy, but poorly trained and educationally limited blacks have been increasingly restricted to the more unstable, low-wage jobs. Affirmative action programs, according to Wilson, have benefited primarily those blacks with good education and training, thus widening the economic division within the black population. Wilson contrasts the improving situation of the black middle class with the worsening situation of what he calls the "black underclass," consisting of "that massive population at the very bottom of the social class ladder plagued by poor education and low-paying, unstable jobs."[22]

The thesis of a split within the black community is still subject to debate, but it deserves our consideration because it appears to fit with the postwar trends in black family life noted above, which appear to be more pronounced among blacks with less education.[23] Figure 4-4 displays the trends from 1940 to 1979 in the marital status of black women aged twenty-five to forty-four with different levels of education, which I use here as an indicator of social class. In 1940 nearly nine out of ten black women in this age range had not finished high school; 6 percent had achieved a high school degree, and an additional 4 percent had completed one or more years of college. But during the postwar years, the educational opportunities for young blacks improved markedly. By 1979 only about one out of three black women aged twenty-five to forty-four didn't have a high school degree; more than four out of ten had finished high school but had not gone on to college, and about one in four had completed one or more years of college. Figure 4-4 shows that the changes in marital status were greater for women without a high school degree than for the increasing numbers who had at least finished high school.

Consider first the upper panel, which charts the percentage married with a husband present. In 1940 black women who had not finished high school were more likely to be currently married than were better-educated black women, but by 1979 the reverse was true. In fact, during the thirty-nine-year interval the percentage of college-educated black women who were currently married decreased by only about 5 percentage points, and the percentage of currently married high-school-educated black women decreased by about 11 percentage points. The decline was much greater for black women who hadn't completed high school, among whom the proportion currently married dropped about 28 percentage points. The lower panel of Figure 4-4 displays the percentage never married. In 1940 the more

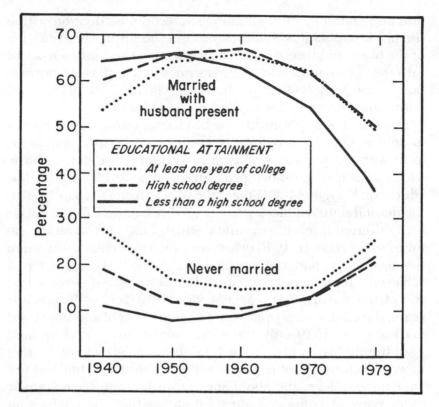

Figure 4-4 Percentage married with husband present and percentage never married of black women aged 25 to 44, by educational attainment, 1940 to 1979. Data for 1940, 1970, and 1979 refer to blacks. Data for 1950 and 1960 refer to nonwhites. (Sources: U.S. Bureau of the Census. *Sixteenth Census of the United States: 1940,* "Population: Educational. Attainment by Economic Characteristics and Marital Status," Table 40; *U.S. Census of Population: 1950,* vol. IV, Special Reports, pt. 5, chap. B, "Education," Table 8; *U.S. Census of Population: 1960,* Subject Reports, Final Report PC(2)-4E, "Marital Status," Table 4; *U.S. Census of Population: 1970,* Subject Reports, Final Report PC(2)-4C, "Marital Status," Table 4; unpublished tabulations from public use tape of March 1979 Current Population Survey. Tabulations by James A. Sweet, Center for Demography and Ecology, University of Wisconsin, Madison.)

education a black woman had, the less likely she was to have ever married, but by 1979 the differences were much smaller. Among those who had at least graduated from high school, the percentage who had never married in 1979 is very similar to the percentage who had never married in 1940. Yet among black women who had not finished high school, the percentage who had never married doubled.

During the same period, of course, the marital status of

whites also was changing. In order to compare the trends for whites and blacks with different levels of education, I have assembled in Table 4-2 comparable information for white and black women aged twenty-five to forty-four. First of all, it can be seen that black-white differences widened between 1940 and 1979 within each category of education. In other words, blacks in general showed more movement away from being currently married than did whites, and blacks in general also showed more movement toward never having married. But Table 4-2 also shows that the gap between blacks and whites increased the most for the less well educated. In 1940 the differences between blacks and whites were virtually the same for those with less than a high school degree as for those who had completed at

Table 4-2. Percentage married with husband present and percentage never married for women aged 25 to 44, by race and educational attainment, 1940 and 1979.

| Educational status | Married, husband present (%) | | | | | |
| | 1940 (%) | | | 1979 (%) | | |
	White[a]	Black	Difference	White	Black	Difference
Less than high school degree	75	64	11	74	36	38
High school degree	73	61	12	81	49	32
At least one year of college	66	54	12	73	49	24
	Never married (%)					
Less than high school degree	11	11	0	7	23	−16
High school degree	20	19	1	6	21	−15
At least one year of college	28	27	1	15	26	−11

Sources: For 1940, U.S. Bureau of the Census, *Sixteenth Census of the United States, 1940: Population; Educational Attainment by Economic Characteristics and Marital Status*, Tables 37 and 40; For 1979, Unpublished tabulations from the public use tape of the March 1979 Current Population Survey.
a. Data for whites in 1940 refer to native white population.

least one year of college. In 1979, on the other hand, the differences were larger among those with less education.

Overall, Figure 4-4 and Table 4-2 suggest, first, that blacks in general became less similar to whites in their marital status during the postwar period (a conclusion also drawn earlier from Figure 4-3 and Table 4-1). Second, the changes were greatest for blacks with less education, especially for the decreasing proportion of blacks with less than a high school degree. If this second proposition is 'true, a substantial portion of the postwar changes in age at marriage and in marital stability among blacks may represent the response of the poorest, most disadvantaged segment of the black population to the social and economic situation they have faced in our cities over the past few decades.

Why should the family patterns of disadvantaged blacks have changed in this way? Several scholars have argued recently that the family patterns that have become common among poor blacks are a rational, adaptive response to their economic situation—perhaps the best response under the circumstances. According to this view, the difficulty of finding stable, decent-paying work makes it difficult for lower-class men and women to hold a marriage together. Consequently, many center their family lives less on marital ties and more on an extended network of kin. Carol Stack, an anthropologist, studied a low-income black neighborhood in the Midwest and found that most residents were part of a complex network of relatives and close friends who exchanged mutual support. When one member of a network needed help with child care or an overdue bill, the other members of the network assisted as best they could. The person who received the assistance was then obligated to help out others in the network.[24] In effect, these kin networks helped to socialize the hardships of poverty, cushioning the inevitable shocks of lower-class life.

But the question still remains as to why stable marital ties seem to be less prevalent among many low-income black families now than was the case just a few decades ago. This question currently is the subject of vigorous and sometimes acrimonious debate. On the one hand, some scholars stress the debilitating effects of high unemployment on marriage. There is some evidence, for example, that the proportion of black families headed by a woman may have risen sharply in the urban North during the depression.[25] Moreover, the postwar unemployment rate for blacks has been much higher than for whites; among young black adults, who are in the prime years for forming families, double-digit unemployment has been the rule rather than the exception. During the 1970s the unemployment rate for black males aged eighteen and nineteen rose from 23 to 30 percent; among black males aged twenty to twenty-four it rose from 13 to 17 percent.[26]

Yet by itself a high level of unemployment is not a fully adequate explanation. During the 1960s the black unemployment rate fell, but the trend toward greater marital instability was still strong.[27] Other scholars believe that the increasing urbanization of blacks, a consequence of the great postwar migration from the rural South to the urban North, might have affected the levels of marital disruption through the 1960s.[28] But the urbanization of blacks has slowed dramatically; beginning in the mid-1970s the number of blacks moving out of central cities exceeded those moving into central cities.[29] The trend toward greater marital instability, however, accelerated in the 1970s.

Still other observers suggest that government social welfare policies may have influenced marital patterns.[30] They point to the expansion since the mid-1960s of such programs as Aid to Families with Dependent Children and food stamps. It is likely, they suggest, that the greater availability and increased benefits of public assistance encouraged or enabled more single-parent families to exist. The empirical evidence isn't entirely consistent, but it suggests that increased welfare benefits may have a modest effect on the proportion of single-parent families.[31] The expansion of welfare, moreover, occurred too recently to account for the more limited pre-1960 trends in family structure. No single explanation, therefore, of the postward trends in marital instability among blacks is entirely satisfactory.

THE CONSEQUENCES OF THE TRENDS

We have seen evidence that in some respects the typical family patterns of black and white Americans have diverged in the postwar period. Perhaps the most fundamental difference is in the role of marriage. I've argued in this book that marriage is still the heart of American family life and that even the increasing age at marriage and the higher divorce rate in recent years are unlikely to dislodge marriage from its central position. This statement, I believe, is true for Americans in general, but the recent trends among blacks suggest a qualification: marriage seems to be less central to the family lives of a substantial segment of the black population than it is to Americans in general. For many blacks, ties to a network of kin may be the more important family bond over the long run. To be sure, kinship ties traditionally have been an important source of support for blacks. But particularly among blacks with less education, there has been a postwar rise in the age at marriage and a sharp decrease in the proportion who are currently married and living with a spouse. Consequently, kin networks appear to be relatively more important, compared to marital ties, than they were in the past. The magnitudes of the increases in age at marriage and in marital instability, as we have seen, are far greater for blacks than the magnitudes of similar trends for whites. Moreover, it appears that for many young black women, the birth of a first child and the beginning of marriage have become two quite separate events. As a result of these and other developments, the proportion of black families maintained by a woman increased sharply during the postwar period.

Commonly used phrases such as "families maintained by a woman" or "single-parent families" can be somewhat misleading, however, when applied to black families. The Bureau of the Census, which provides these statistics, defines a family as two or more individuals related by blood or marriage who reside in the same household. This definition assumes that all of the relevant members of a family share the same household. Studies of low-income black families by Stack and others, however, show that a single parent's family often consists of a number of kin spread over several households—a mother, an aunt, a brother, an in-law, and so forth, who share and exchange goods, services, and emotional support. The census figures do indicate the increasing frequency of broken ties between fathers and mothers and between husbands and wives, but they can leave the mistaken impression that most black single parents and their children belong to unstable families. In fact, according to most accounts, the extended kin networks characteristic of many low-income blacks provide a stable, functioning family environment on which the members of the network can rely.[32] Household composition may change, but the network tends to remain intact.

Despite its strengths, this kind of family structure sometimes can pose difficulties for its members. Group loyalty, the essence of the strength of the family networks, can conflict with the goals of individuals. For instance, it may be difficult for a single person or a couple to amass enough resources to advance their own standard of living because of their obligations to others in the network. When a young woman studied by Stack wanted to marry, the members of her network discouraged her from doing so. Her contribution was valuable to the others, and they feared she would withdraw from the network if she married. As a matter of fact, during the study she did marry and, recognizing that the demands of the network might conflict with the demands of her marriage, that evening she left the state with her husband. In another instance an older couple unexpectedly inherited $1,500. At first they decided to use the money as a down payment on a house, but others in their network soon made a series of requests for money that couldn't be refused. Several relatives needed train fare to attend a funeral; another needed $25 so her phone wouldn't be turned off; a sister faced eviction because of overdue rent. The local welfare office also helped take the surplus away by cutting the couple's children off welfare temporarily. Within six weeks the windfall was gone.[33] Stack's study suggests that it is difficult for anyone in these networks to raise his or her level of living until everyone in the network is able to raise their level. A person who marries or gets a job and wishes to move up the social ladder may be forced to leave the network, but this is a risky step, not to be taken lightly, given the high rate of marital dissolution and the insecure nature of low-wage work. Although the family networks among low-income blacks ease the burdens of poverty, they may also make it difficult for individuals to rise out of poverty.

Moreover, even these supportive family networks can't eliminate the economic hardships that beset many black single mothers and their children. I discussed in chapter 3 the economic difficulties that single parents face, and I noted that the difficulties are typically much worse for single mothers than for single fathers. These statements hold for blacks as well as whites. Suzanne M. Bianchi and Reynolds Farley reported that between 1960 and 1976 the per capita income in black and white households maintained by women increased much less rapidly than in households maintained by men or in husband-wife households. Consequently, blacks living in households maintained by women fell further behind economically, while the proportion of all blacks living in these financially strapped households rose.[34] These figures don't take into account the transfers of goods and services across households by members of family networks, but they suggest that the economic situation of black single parents and their children has deteriorated relative to the advances made by blacks and whites in other kinds of families.

We still don't know the long-term consequences of the decreasing relative importance of marital ties among many low-income blacks because, as I have shown, this is a fairly recent phenomenon. A family structure characterized by a strong network of kin but fragile ties between fathers and mothers apparently was much less common among blacks as recently as 1960. Whether this new family structure has become firmly entrenched remains to be seen. Meanwhile the statistics and studies I have reviewed show a sharp divergence in recent decades between blacks and whites in the typical patterns of marriage. And on closer examination it appears that the changes have been greatest among lower-class black families. The emerging family system among lower-class blacks suggests that some are becoming even less integrated into the mainstream of American life than ever before.

Appendix 1
Constructing Figure 1-1

Figure 1-1 shows the first quartile, median, and third quartile ages at first marriage for five birth cohorts of women: 1910 to 1914, 1920 to 1924, 1930 to 1934, 1940 to 1944, and 1950 to 1954. The first quartile is the age at which one-fourth of all the members of the cohort who ever married had already done so. The median is the age at which half of the ever-married had done so; the third quartile is the age at which three-fourths of the ever-married had done so. Information on the four older cohorts was obtained from the June 1975 supplement to the Current Population Survey, as reported in U.S. Bureau of the Census, Current Population Reports, series P-20, no. 297, "Number, Timing, and Duration of Marriages and Divorces in the United States: June 1975" (Washington: U.S. Government Printing Office, 1976). The report is based on retrospective marital histories supplied by respondents in this national sample of about 50,000 households. Only women who survived to 1975, obviously, were represented in the survey. Since married persons have a lower mortality rate than unmarried persons, the reports may slightly misrepresent the cohort histories, especially for women born early in the century. For this reason, I did not construct estimates for cohorts earlier than 1910 to 1914, whose members were sixty-one to sixty-five in 1975.

In the three older cohorts almost everyone who would ever marry had done so by 1975. For these three I calculated the first quartile, median, and third quartile ages at marriage from Table 2 of the census report. I used linear interpolation between the single-year-of-age categories listed in Table 2. There was one exception to this procedure: the third quartile for the 1910 to 1914 cohort fell in a five-year category, ages twenty-five to twenty-nine. Since the number of women marrying at twenty-five to twenty-nine is not uniformly distributed by single year of age, linear interpolation was not appropriate. Instead I used nonlinear interpolation based on the single-year-of-age distribution of brides in 1940 who were between the ages of twenty-five to twenty-nine. For all three cohorts, my calculations of the median age at marriage matched the census estimates presented in Table J of the report.

The procedure was almost the same for the 1940 to 1944 cohort. A few of these women will marry for the first time after 1975, that is, after reaching ages forty-one to forty-five. I estimated the number who will marry after those ages based on the experiences of slightly older cohorts. I then calculated the first quartile, median, and third quartile ages at marriage as I did for the older cohorts.

For the four older cohorts my estimates of age at first marriage were:

Cohort	First quartile	Median	Third quartile
1910 to 1914	18.9	21.8	25.8
1920 to 1924	18.9	21.2	24.2
1930 to 1934	18.4	20.3	22.8
1940 to 1944	18.5	20.3	22.8

For the 1950 to 1954 cohort, I estimated the median and first and third quartile ages at marriage from unpublished tabulations kindly provided by Maurice J. Moore and Carolyn C. Rogers of the U.S. Bureau of the Census. Moore and Rogers have analyzed data on date of birth and date of first marriage which were collected from women in the June 1978 Current Population Survey. They calculated the cumulative probabilities of remaining single at each age for birth cohorts of women from 1919 to 1957. The results were reported for selected cohorts in their paper, "Some New Measurements of First Marriage, 1954 to 1977," presented at the annual meeting of the Population Association of America, Philadelphia, April 28, 1979. For women born in the 1940s and 1950s, Moore and Rogers projected probabilities of remaining single at later ages based on the actual probabilities of slightly older cohorts.

From their figures I assembled the actual probabilities of remaining single for the 1950 to 1954 cohort at each age from fifteen to twenty-four. At age twenty-four the probability of still remaining single was .2878. Using their projection method, I then estimated that for this cohort the probability of still remaining single at age forty will be .0805. Thus an estimated 92 percent of the cohort will marry by age forty if this projection method is accurate—that is, if the experiences of slightly older cohorts can be used to predict what will happen to this cohort in the future. An additional 2 percent of the 1950 to 1954 cohort are likely to marry for the first time after age forty, according to the reports of older women in the June 1975 Current Population Survey. Thus my best estimate is that 94 percent of all the women born between 1950 and 1954 will eventually marry. Using this lifetime total and the probabilities of remaining single at ages fifteen through twenty-four from the Moore and Rogers tabulations, one can calculate estimated median and quartile ages at marriage from the following table. Column I gives the cumulative proportion ever married for the entire 1950 to 1954 cohort of women, and column II gives the cumulative proportion ever married for all women in that cohort who will marry eventually (equals column I divided by 0.94).

Age	I	II
15	.0077	.0082
16	.0349	.0371
17	.0845	.0888
18	.1812	.1928
19	.3036	.3230
20	.4177	.4444
21	.5160	.5489
22	.5976	.6357
23	.6609	.7031
24	.7122	.7577

These proportions can be considered to be cumulative through the midpoint of each age category; then linear interpolation of column II yields a first quartile of 18.9, a median of 21.0, and a third quartile of 24.4. In order to check this procedure, I calculated the median and quartile ages at marriage for the 1930 to 1934 cohort from the Moore and Rogers data, and these estimates matched those obtained from the Bureau of the Census report on the June 1975 survey discussed above.

Appendix 2
Constructing Figure 1-5

Figure 1-5 displays estimates of the proportion of marriages begun in each year between 1867 and 1973 which will end in divorce. The estimates for 1867 to 1949 are taken from Samuel H. Preston and John McDonald, "The Incidence of Divorce within Cohorts of American Marriages Contracted Since the Civil War," *Demography* 16 (Feb. 1979): 1–25, whose estimates are based on vital registration and census data. Preston and McDonald estimated the lifetime proportions divorcing for marriages surviving to 1970 by assuming that 1969 divorce and death rates will continue to hold in the future.

The data for 1950 to 1973 are taken from projections by James Weed published in U.S. National Center for Health Statistics, Vital and Health Statistics, series 3, no. 19, "National Estimates of Marital Dissolution and Survivorship" (Washington, U.S. Government Printing Office, 1980). These projections are based on the actual experiences of marriage cohorts through 1977, and they assume that the divorce and death rates of the 1976 to 1977 period will continue to hold in the future. Since the 1976–1977 rates of divorce were higher than the 1969 rates, Weed's projection for 1950 is slightly higher than Preston and McDonald's projection for 1950 (.295 and .271, respectively). Thus there is a slight discontinuity introduced by changing in 1950 to Weed's more up-to-date projections. I have smoothed the data by plotting three-year moving averages in 1949 and 1950.

The solid curve in Figure 1-5 is the result of fitting a second-degree polynomial on time to the projected proportions by ordinary least squares regression. A similar procedure for 1867 to 1964 can be found in Preston and McDonald. This curve fits the data excellently: the fitted values account for 99 percent of the variance in the projected proportions. The regression equation is:

$ln\ p = -2.901 + .02272T - .00002222T^2, (R^2 = .993),$

where p is the predicted proportion divorcing, T is year minus 1867, and ln is the natural logarithm.

Appendix 3
Estimating the Total Dissolution Rate for Marriages in 1978

The total dissolution rate for marriages in a given year is the sum of the rates of dissolution by death and by divorce. Kingsley Davis calculated the total dissolution rate per 1,000 existing marriages for five-year intervals between 1860 and 1970. (See Kingsley Davis, "The American Family in Relation to Demographic Change," in Charles F. Westoff and Robert Parke, Jr., Commission on Population Growth and the American Future, Research Reports, vol. 1, *Demographic and Social Aspects of Population Growth* [Washington: U.S. Government Printing Office, 1972], Table 8.) In order to calculate the rate for the latest available year, one needs three pieces of information: the number of existing marriages, the number of divorces, and the number of deaths of married persons. The first two are readily available. For 1978 the number of existing marriages was obtained from U.S. Bureau of the Census, Current Population Reports, series P-20, no. 338, "Marital Status and Living Arrangements: March 1978" (Washington: U.S. Government Printing Office, 1979). In order to be consistent with Davis's calculations, I took the number of married men (spouse present and spouse absent) as the indicator of the number of existing marriages. The number of divorces in 1978 is reported in U.S. National Center for Health Statistics, Monthly Vital Statistics Report, vol. 27, no. 13, *Annual Summary for the United States, 1978* (Washington: U.S. Government Printing Office, 1970).

The problem, however, is that since 1961 death rates for married persons have not been reported, only death rates for all persons. Yet we know that married persons have somewhat lower death rates than unmarried persons. Davis estimated the number of deaths to married persons for 1965 and 1970; I have done so for 1978, using the following procedure. I compared the death rates for married persons by age and sex in 1960 with the death rates by age and sex for all persons in 1960. From this comparison I calculated the ratio of the death rate for married persons to the rate for all persons in each age-sex group. These ratios were typically in the range of 0.8 to 0.9. I then multiplied the death rates for all persons by age and sex in 1978 by the corresponding ratios. Thus I adjusted the total death rates in 1978 to reflect the somewhat lower risk of death for married people. This adjustment assumes that the ratio of the death rates of married persons to all persons has stayed the same for each age-sex group between 1960 and 1978, an assumption that seems reasonable for the purposes of this chapter. I then multiplied each adjusted death rate by the number of married people in the appropriate age-sex group (obtained from Current Population Reports, series P-20, no. 338), yielding an estimate of 906,300 deaths to married persons in 1978.

The figures used in calculating the total rate of dissolution, then, were as follows:

Deaths to married persons in 1978	906,300
Divorces in 1978	1,128,000
Existing marriages in 1978	50,167,000
Deaths per 1,000 existing marriages	18.1
Divorces per 1,000 existing marriages	22.4
Total dissolutions per 1,000 existing marriages	40.5

Appendix 4
Constructing Figure 3-1

Figure 3-1 charts the lifetime marriage and divorce experiences of three cohorts of women: those born in 1910 to 1914, 1930 to 1934, and 1950 to 1954. For the two older cohorts I assembled estimates of the proportions ever marrying, ever divorcing, ever remarrying following a divorce, and ever divorcing a second time. For the 1950 to 1954 cohort I gathered estimates for the proportions experiencing the first three of these four events. I also assembled data on the actual or projected median age at which these events occurred (or will occur) for each cohort, although this information is not shown in Figure 3-1.

The estimates for the 1910 to 1914 cohort all were obtained from U.S. Bureau of the Census, Current Population Reports, series P-20, no. 297. This report contains data from retrospective marital histories obtained from a national sample in 1975; a more detailed description of these data and their limitations appears in Appendix 1. The major limitation is that women who survived until 1975 may not be fully representative of all women born into this cohort. The lifetime histories of marrying, divorcing, and remarrying following a divorce were virtually complete for this cohort by 1975; the relevant percentages and medians were obtained from summary tables in the census report. There was, however, one exception: I estimated the median age at redivorce from the detailed age distribution in Table 2. Since few women in this cohort divorced twice, my estimate—fifty years of age—should be regarded as an approximate figure only.

I used the same source to construct the estimates for the 1930 to

1934 cohort, but because this cohort is still marrying and divorcing, some of the figures are projections. In its report the Bureau of the Census calculated projections of the proportion of all ever-married persons in this cohort whose first marriages will end in divorce and all ever remarried persons whose second marriages will end in divorce, based on the recent experience of slightly older cohorts. I used a similar method, based on the same data, to project the lifetime proportions of the divorced who will ever remarry, as well as the estimated median ages at the onset of divorce, remarriage, and redivorce. These projections may underestimate the lifetime levels of divorce and redivorce if the women in this cohort divorce at a higher rate in their forties and fifties than did earlier cohorts. Nevertheless, much of the marrying and divorcing in this cohort had already occurred by 1975, so the projections should provide us with reasonably accurate estimates for cross-cohort comparisons.

I selected the 1950 to 1954 cohort as representative of the postwar baby boom cohorts because, as I described in Appendix 1, a detailed projection of the proportion still single at each age could be calculated for this cohort from tabulations by Moore and Rogers. Using the Moore and Rogers tabulations and 1975 census data, I estimated that about 94 percent of women born in 1950 to 1954 will ever marry and that the median age at marriage will be 21.0 (see Appendix 1). Projecting the proportion of these marriages that will end in divorce is more difficult, since many of these divorces have not yet occurred. The estimated median age at marrige suggests that the most typical years of first marriage for this cohort were the early and mid-1970s. The U.S. National Center for Health Statistics recently projected that 47.4 percent of all first marriages begun in 1974 would end in divorce if the divorce and death rates prevailing in 1975 were to continue. (See U.S. National Center for Health Statistics, Vital and Health Statistics, series 3, no. 19, "National Estimates of Marital Dissolution and Survivorship," [Washington, U.S. Government Printing Office, 1980.]) I have taken this estimate as the best available projection of the lifetime percentage of first marriages ending in divorce for the 1950 to 1954 cohort.

According to the reports of older cohorts in the 1975 census survey, about three out of four divorced women remarry eventually. As I noted in the text, the remarriage rate rose sharply after 1940 but has fallen since the 1960s. In constructing Figure 3-1 I have assumed that three out of four of the divorced women in the 1950 to 1954 cohort will remarry. I have not attempted to estimate the level of redivorce for this cohort. My estimates of the median ages at divorce and remarriage also are necessarily rough. The median ages at divorce and re-marriage appear to have been dropping in recent years, but the drop is exaggerated because the divorce and remarriage experiences of recent cohorts are incomplete. I have estimated the median age at divorce as thirty and the median age at remarriage as thirty-three for the 1950 to 1954 cohort. These figures are slightly lower than the projections for the 1930 to 1934 cohort.

In sum, the estimates for the most recent cohort in Figure 3-1 are approximate, and they make assumptions about future divorce and death rates which may not hold. Yet these estimates are unlikely to be too far off the mark. By 1978, for example, nearly three-quarters of the women born in 1950 to 1954 had married, and the lifetime proportions marrying for this cohort can be estimated with confidence to within a few percentage points. Moreover, we know already that there has been a great deal of divorce among those marrying in the early 1970s; as I mentioned in the text, one-fourth of all marriages begun in 1970 had ended in divorce by 1977. As we enter the 1980s the divorce rate is still rising, albeit more slowly; projections based on 1975 levels of divorce still seem to be plausible guides to the future. They may even underestimate lifetime levels of divorce. The point of constructing Figure 3-1 is not to provide a set of precise estimates for all time, but rather to compare graphically the experiences of three cohorts. For this purpose the estimates described here for the 1950 to 1954 cohort should serve us adequately.

Estimates (*—plotted in Figure 3-1)	1910–1914	1930–1934	1950–1954
A.* Percent who ever marry	93.9	96.1	94.0
B. Percent of ever-married who ever divorce	15.8	26.0	47.4
C.* Percent of cohort who ever divorce (= A × B)	14.8	25.0	44.6
D. Percent of ever-divorced who ever remarry	81.2	80.5	75.0
E.* Percent of cohort who ever remarry (= A × B × D)	12.0	20.1	33.5
F. Percent of ever-remar-			

	ried who ever redivorce	12.0	26.0	—
G.*	Percent of cohort who ever redivorce (= A × B × D × F)	1.4	5.2	—
H.	Median age at first marriage	21.8	20.3	21.0
I.	Median age at divorce	31.2	30.8	30.0
J.	Median age at remarriage	34.9	33.7	33.0
K.	Median age at redivorce	50	42.4	—

Notes

Introduction

1. Quoted in Herman Lantz, Martin Schultz, and Mary O'Hara, "The Changing American Family from the Preindustrial to the Industrial Period: A Final Report," *American Sociological Review* 42 (June 1977): 406–421, at p. 413.

2. See, for example, Mary Jo Bane, *Here to Stay: American Families in the Twentieth Century* (New York: Basic Books, 1976).

3. Christopher Lasch, "Life in the Therapeutic State," *New York Review of Books* 27 (June 12, 1980): 24–32, at p. 31.

1. The Trends

1. Norman B. Ryder, "The Family in Developed Countries," *Scientific American* 231 (Sept. 1974): 122–132.

2. U.S. Bureau of the Census, *Historical Statistics of the United States, Colonial Times to 1970,* bicentennial ed., Pt. 1 (Washington: U.S. Government Printing Office, 1975) p. 49.

3. Information on the women born in 1950 to 1954 is less complete than for women born earlier, but about three-fourths of them had already married. For this cohort I have relied on estimates by Maurice J. Moore and Carolyn C. Rogers of the proportions marrying at each age. For details of the construction of Figure 1-1, see Appendix 1.

4. U.S. Bureau of the Census, Current Population Reports, series P-20, no. 297, "Number, Timing, and Duration of Marriages and Divorces in the United States: June 1975" (Washington: U.S. Government Printing Office, 1976).

5. Kingsley Davis, "The American Family in Relation to Demographic Change," in Charles F. Westoff and Robert Parke, Jr., eds., Commission on

Population Growth and the American Future, Research Reports, vol. 1, *Demographic and Social Aspects of Population Growth* (Washington: U.S. Government Printing Office, 1972), pp. 236–265.

6. Davis, "American Family."

7. Another trend in the timing of marriage is, as Figure 1-2 shows, that the percentages never married for men aged twenty to twenty-four have become more similar over time to those for women in the same age group. This reflects the lessening of the age gap between spouses in the twentieth century. Among people born in 1900 to 1904, the median age of men at first marriage was about four years more than the median age among women. By the time the depression cohort came of age, this difference had been reduced: for those born between 1930 and 1934, the difference was less than three years. For the baby boom cohort, the differences is likely to be about two years. (See Current Population Reports, series P-20, no. 297.)

8. U.S. Bureau of the Census, Current Population Reports, series P-20, no. 349, "Marital Status and Living Arrangements: March 1979" (Washington: U.S. Government Printing Office, 1980). Even these figures may underestimate the change because they compare decennial census data for 1970 with Current Population Survey data for 1979. James A. Sweet, who examined Current Population Survey data in 1970 and later in the decade found evidence that the number of cohabiting persons may have more than tripled in the 1970s. See James A. Sweet, "Estimates of Levels, Trends, and Characteristics of the 'Living Together' Population from the Current Population Survey," Working Paper 79–49, Center for Demography and Ecology, University of Wisconsin, Madison, 1979.

9. Richard R. Clayton and Harwin L. Voss, "Shacking Up: Cohabitation in the 1970s," *Journal of Marriage and the Family* 39 (May 1977): 273–283.

10. Paul C. Glick and Graham B. Spanier, "Married and Unmarried Cohabitation in the United States," *Journal of Marriage and the Family* 42 (Feb. 1980): 19–30.

11. Glick and Spanier, "Married and Unmarried Cohabitation."

12. Ibiathaj Arafat and Betty Yorburg, "On Living Together without Marriage," *Journal of Sex Research* 9 (May 1973): 97–106.

13. Clayton and Voss, "Shacking Up."

14. Donald W. Bower and Victor A. Christopherson, "University Student Cohabitation: A Regional Comparison of Selected Attitudes and Behavior," *Journal of Marriage and the Family* 39 (Aug. 1977): 447–453.

15. Clayton and Voss, "Shacking Up."

16. Jan Trost, "Dissolution of Cohabitation and Marriage in Sweden," *Journal of Divorce* 2 (Summer 1979): 415–421; and Jan Trost, "A Renewed Social Institution: Non-Marital Cohabitation," *Acta Sociologica* 21, no. 4 (1978): 303–315.

17. Louis Roussel and Odile Bourguignon, *Générations Nouvelles et Mariage Traditionnel* (Paris: Presses Universitaires de France, 1978).

18. Trost, "Dissolution of Cohabitation and Marriage."

19. Eleanor D. Macklin, "Nonmarital Heterosexual Cohabitation," *Marriage and Family Review* 1 (March/April 1978): 1–12.

20. Most notably in *Marvin v. Marvin*. See Macklin, "Nonmarital Heterosexual Cohabitation," for a discussion of these cases.

21. See Macklin, "Nonmarital Heterosexual Cohabitation," for a summary and critique of these views.

22. Larry L. Bumpass and James A. Sweet, "Differentials in Marital Instability: 1970," *American Sociological Review* 37 (Dec. 1972): 754–766.

23. Norman B. Ryder, "Components of Temporal Variations in American Fertility," in Robert W. Hiorns, ed., *Demographic Patterns in Developed Societies* (London: Taylor and Francis, 1980), pp. 15–54.

24. Ryder, "Components of Temporal Variations."

25. In order to estimate the fertility of the more recent cohorts, Ryder assumed that age-parity-specific birth rates will remain the same as they were in 1975.

26. Ryder, "Components of Temporal Variations."

27. See Appendix 2.

28. See Appendix 2 for details about how this curve was fitted to the proportions.

29. U.S. National Center for Health Statistics, Vital and Health Statistics, series 3, no. 19, "National Estimates of Marital Dissolution and Survivorship" (Washington: U.S. Government Printing Office, 1980); U.S. National Center for Health Statistics, Vital and Health Statistics, series 21, no. 34, "Divorces by Marriage Cohort" (Washington: U.S. Government Printing Office, 1979).

30. Davis, "American Family"; see also Mary Jo Bane, *Here to Stay: American Families in the Twentieth Century* (New York: Basic Books, 1976).

31. See Appendix 3.

32. See Appendix 3.

33. Current Population Reports, series P-20, no. 297.

34. Larry Bumpass and Ronald R. Rindfuss, "Children's Experience of Marital Disruption," *American Journal of Sociology* 85 (July 1979): 49–65.

35. Current Population Reports, series P-20, no. 349.

36. U.S. Bureau of the Census, Current Population Reports, series P-23, no. 107, "Families Maintained by Female Householders 1970–79" (Washington: U.S. Government Printing Office, 1980), Table 4.

37. James A. Sweet, "The Living Arrangements of Separated, Widowed, and Divorced Mothers," *Demography* 9 (Feb. 1972): 143–157.

38. Bumpass and Rindfuss, "Children's Experience of Marital Disruption."

39. U.S. Bureau of the Census, *Census of Population, 1970,* Subject Reports, Final Report PC(2)-4B, "Persons by Family Characteristics" (Washington: U.S. Government Printing Office, 1973).

40. James McCarthy, "A Comparison of the Probability of the Dissolution of First and Second Marriages," *Demography* 15 (Aug. 1978): 345–359.

41. Current Population Reports, series P-20, no. 349.

42. Current Population Reports, series P-20, no. 349; and U.S. Bureau of the Census, *Census of Population: 1960,* Final Report PC(2)-4B, "Persons by Family Characteristics" (Washington: U.S. Government Printing Office, 1964).

43. John Demos, *A Little Commonwealth: Family Life in Plymouth Colony* (New York: Oxford University Press, 1970).

44. Paul H. Jacobson, *American Marriage and Divorce* (New York: Rinehart, 1959).

45. U.S. National Center for Health Statistics, Monthly Vital Statistics Report, vol. 29, no. 6, supplement (1), Advance Report, "Final Marriage Statistics, 1978" (Washington: U.S. Government Printing Office, 1980), Table 3.

46. Center for Health Statistics, "Final Marriage Statistics, 1978;" and Jacobson, *American Marriage and Divorce.*

47. Arthur J. Norton and Paul C. Glick, "Marital Instability in America: Past, Present, and Future," in George Levinger and Oliver C. Moles, eds., *Divorce and Separation: Context, Causes, and Consequences* (New York: Basic Books, 1979), pp. 6–19.

48. See Current Population Reports, series P-20, no. 297 for data on age at remarriage by cohort.

49. In recent years, however, the percentage of all divorces involving children has dropped from the peak levels of the 1960s because of the falling birth rate. The percentage was 45 percent in 1953; it rose to 62 percent in 1964; and it has since fallen to 57 percent. See U.S. National Center for Health Statistics, Vital Statistics of the United States, 1975, vol. 3, *Marriage and Divorce* (Washington: U.S. Government Printing Office, 1979).

50. Paul C. Glick, "Children of Divorced Parents in Demographic Perspective," *Journal of Social Issues* 4 (1979): 170–182.

51. See Andrew Cherlin, "Remarriage as an Incomplete Institution," *American Journal of Sociology* 84 (Nov. 1978): 634–650.

52. Center for Health Statistics, "National Estimates of Marriage Dissolution and Survivorship."

2. The Explanations

1. Harold F. Dorn, "Pitfalls in Population Forecasts and Projections," *Journal of the American Statistical Association* 45 (Sept. 1950): 311–334.

2. U.S. Bureau of the Census, Current Population Reports, series P-20, no. 349, "Marital Status and Living Arrangements: March 1979" (Washington, U.S. Government Printing Office, 1980), Table A.

3. U.S. Bureau of the Census, *Historical Statistics of the United States, Colonial Times to 1970*, bicentennial.ed., pt. 1, series B-11 (Washington: U.S. Government Printing Office, 1975).

4. See, for example, Betty Friedan, *The Feminine Mystique* (New York: W.W. Norton, 1963), chap. 8.

5. See John R. Seeley, R. Alexander Sim, and Elizabeth W. Loosley, *Crestwood Heights* (New York: Basic Books, 1956); A. C. Spectorsky, *The Exurbanites* (New York: Lippincott, 1955); and William H. Whyte, Jr., *The Organization Man* (New York: Simon and Schuster, 1956).

6. Norman B. Ryder, "Recent Trends and Group Differences in Fertility," in Charles F. Westoff, ed., *Toward the End of Growth* (Englewood Cliffs, N.J.: Prentice-Hall, 1973) pp. 57–68; and Judith Blake and Prithwis Das Gupta, "Reply," *Population and Development Review* 4 (June 1978): 326–329.

7. See Bennett M. Berger, *Working-Class Suburb* (Berkeley: University of California Press, 1971); and Herbert J. Gans, *The Levittowners* (New York: Random House, 1967).

8. John Modell, "Normative Aspects of American Marriage Timing Since World War II," *Journal of Family History* 5 (Summer 1980): 210–234.

9. Modell, "Normative Aspects."

10. Mirra Komarovsky, *The Unemployed Man and His Family* (New York: Dryden Press, 1940), p. 98.

11. Komarovsky, *Unemployed Man*, pp. 100–101.

12. Glen H. Elder, Jr., *Children of the Great Depression* (Chicago: University of Chicago Press, 1974).

13. Richard A. Easterlin, "What Will 1984 Be Like? Socioeconomic Implications of Recent Twists in the Age Structure," *Demography* 15 (Nov. 1978): 397–432; and Richard A. Easterlin, *Birth and Fortune: The Impact of Numbers on Personal Welfare* (New York: Basic Books, 1980).

14. Richard A. Easterlin, *Population, Labor Force, and Long Swings in Economic Growth* (New York: Columbia University Press, 1968) p. 124; and Komarovsky, *Unemployed Man.*

15. "Age" explanations constitute a third general class: those that refer to the effects of the aging process. An older population, for example, will produce fewer babies each year than will a younger population. In the case of marriage and divorce since World War II, however, large changes have occurred in the experiences of comparable age groups; married men and women in their twenties in 1980 had a much higher probability of divorcing than did married men and women in their twenties in 1960. Therefore, no age explanation can account for more than a small part of the changes in marriage and divorce in recent years.

16. Other cohort-based explanations for postwar changes in family patterns have been proposed recently by Jean Bourgeois-Pichat, "La Baisse Actuelle de la Fécondité en Europe S'Inscrit-elle dans le Modèle de la Transition Démographique?" *Population* 34 (March/April 1979): 267–306; and Elwood Carlson, "Divorce Rate Fluctuation as a Cohort Phenomenon," *Population Studies* 33 (Nov. 1979): 523–536.

17. Maurice M. MacDonald and Ronald R. Rindfuss, "Earnings, Relative Income, and Family Formation, Part I: Marriage," unpublished manuscript, Center for Demography and Ecology, University of Wisconsin, Madison, 1980; and Ronald R. Rindfuss and Maurice M. MacDonald, "Earnings, Relative Income, and Family Formation, Part II: Fertility," unpublished manuscript, University of North Carolina at Chapel Hill, 1980.

18. Abbott L. Ferriss, *Indicators of Trends in the Status of American Women* (New York: Russell Sage Foundation, 1971), pp. 348–349.

19. Charles F. Westoff, "Marriage and Fertility in the Developed Countries," *Scientific American* 239 (Dec. 1978): 51–57, at p. 53.

20. Gerald C. Wright, Jr., and Dorothy N. Stetson, "The Impact of No-Fault Divorce Law Reform on Divorce in American States," *Journal of Marriage and the Family* 40 (Aug. 1978): 575–580.

21. Wright and Stetson, "Impact of No-Fault Divorce Law Reform."

22. U.S. Bureau of the Census, Current Population Reports, series P-20, no. 297, "Number, Timing, and Duration of Marriages and Divorces in the United States: June 1975" (Washington: U.S. Government Printing Office, 1976).

23. Valerie Kincade Oppenheimer, *The Female Labor Force in the United States*, Population Monograph Series, no. 5 (Berkeley: Institute of International Studies, 1970); and U.S. Bureau of Labor Statistics, "Multi-Earner Families Increase," press release no. USDL 79–747, October 31, 1979.

24. William P. Butz and Michael P. Ward, "Completed Fertility and its Timing: An Economic Analysis of U.S. Experience Since World War II" Rand Corporation, R-2285-NICHD, (April 1978); and William P. Butz and Michael P. Ward, "The Emergence of Countercyclical U.S. Fertility," *American Economic Review* 69 (June 1979): 318–328.

25. Oppenheimer, *Female Labor Force.*

26. Easterlin, *Birth and Fortune.* For a discussion of explanations for the rise in female labor force participation, see Ralph E. Smith, "The Movement of Women into the Labor Force," in Ralph E. Smith, ed., *The Subtle Revolution: Women at Work* (Washington: Urban Institute, 1979) pp. 1–29.

27. Samuel H. Preston and Alan Thomas Richards, "The Influence of Women's Work Opportunities on Marriage Rates," *Demography* 12 (May 1975): 209–222; and Alan Freiden, "The United States Marriage Market," *Journal of Political Economy* 82, pt. II (March/April 1974): S34–S53.

28. Andrew Cherlin, "Postponing Marriage: The Influence of Young Women's Work Expectations," *Journal of Marriage and the Family* 42 (May 1980): 355–365.

29. Arthur W. Calhoun, *A Social History of the American Family,* vol. 3 (1919; reprint ed., New York: Barnes and Noble, 1960); Willard Waller, *The Family: A Dynamic Interpretation* (New York: Dryden, 1938); William J. Goode, *World Revolution and Family Patterns* (New York: Free Press, 1963); and Carl N. Degler, *At Odds: Women and the Family in America from the Revolution to the Present* (New York: Oxford University Press, 1980).

30. For a discussion of these other characteristics, see Andrew Cherlin, "The Effect of Children on Marital Dissolution," *Demography* 14 (Aug. 1977): 265–272; and Larry L. Bumpass and James A. Sweet, "Differentials in Marital Instability: 1970," *American Sociological Review* 37 (Dec. 1972): 754–766.

31. Heather L. Ross and Isabel V. Sawhill, *Time of Transition: The Growth of Families Headed by Women* (Washington: Urban Institute, 1975); Andrew Cherlin, "Work Life and Marital Dissolution," in George Levinger and Oliver C. Moles, eds., *Divorce and Separation: Context, Causes, and Consequences* (New York: Basic Books, 1979); pp. 151–166; and Michael T. Hannan, Nancy Brandon Tuma, and Lyle P. Groeneveld, "Income and Independence Effects on Marital Dissolution: Results from the Seattle and Denver Income-Maintenance Experiments," *American Journal of Sociology* 84 (Nov. 1978): 611–633. But for results that question the independence effect of wives' income, see Frank L. Mott and Sylvia F. Moore, "Marital Disruption: Causes and Consequences," in Frank L. Mott et al., eds., *Years for Decision,* vol. 4 (Columbus: Center for Human Resource Research, Ohio State University, 1977) pp. 207–256.

32. Easterlin, *Birth and Fortune.*

33. See footnote 17.

34. Charles F Westoff and Norman B. Ryder, *The Contraceptive Revolution* (Princeton: Princeton University Press, 1977); and Charles F. Westoff and Elise F. Jones, "Patterns of Aggregate and Individual Changes in Contraceptive Practice, United States, 1965–1975," U.S. National Center for Health Statistics, Vital and Health Statistics, series 3, no. 17 (Washington: U.S. Government Printing Office, June 1979).

35. Judith Blake and Prithwis Das Gupta, "Reproductive Motivation Versus Contraceptive Technology: Is Recent American Experience an Exception?" *Population and Development Review* 1 (Dec. 1975): 229–249; and Norman B. Ryder, "On the Time Series of American Fertility," and Blake and Das Gupta, "Reply," both in *Population and Development Review* 4 (June 1978): 322–329.

36. See, for example, Easterlin, *Birth and Fortune,* pp. 55–57.

37. See James C. Cramer, "Fertility and Female Employment: Problems of Causal Direction," *American Sociological Review* 45 (April 1980): 167–190.

38. Hugh Carter and Paul C. Glick, *Marriage and Divorce: A Social and Economic Study,* rev. ed., (Cambridge, Mass.: Harvard University Press, 1976).

39. Preston and Richards, "Influence of Women's Work Opportunities."

40. Easterlin, *Birth and Fortune.*

41. See Charles F. Westoff, "Marriage and Fertility in the Developed Countries," *Scientific American* 239 (Dec. 1978): 51-57; Valerie Kincade Oppenheimer, "Structural Sources of Economic Pressure for Wives to Work: An Analytic Framework," *Journal of Family History* 4 (Summer 1979): 177-197; and Butz and Ward, "Completed Fertility and Its Timing."

42. Andrew Cherlin and Pamela Barnhouse Walters, "Trends in United States Men's and Women's Sex-Role Attitudes," *American Sociological Review* 46 (Aug. 1981): in press.

43. Karen Oppenheim Mason, John L. Czajka, and Sara Arber, "Change in U.S. Women's Sex-Role Attitudes, 1964-1974," *American Sociological Review* 41 (Aug. 1976): 573-596; Beverly Duncan and Otis Dudley Duncan, *Sex Typing and Social Roles: A Research Report* (New York: Academic Press, 1978); and Cherlin and Walters, "Trends in Sex-Role Attitudes."

44. See, for example, Westoff, "Marriage and Fertility."

45. Valerie Kincade Oppenheimer, "The Easterlin Hypothesis: Another Aspect of the Echo to Consider," *Population and Development Review* 2 (1976): 433-457; and Oppenheimer, "Structural Sources of Economic Pressure for Wives to Work."

46. U.S. National Center for Health Statistics, Monthly Vital Statistics Report, Provisional Statistics, vol. 28, no. 12, "Births, Marriages, Divorces, and Deaths for 1979" (Washington: U.S. Government Printing Office, March 1980).

47. For a review of the postwar trends in women's labor force participation in Western Europe and the New World, see Judith Blake, "The Changing Status of Women in the Developed Countries," *Scientific American* 231 (Sept. 1974): 137-148.

48. Michael B. Katz, *The People of Hamilton, Canada West: Family and Class in a Mid-Nineteenth-Century City* (Cambridge, Mass.: Harvard University Press, 1975); p. 292.

3. The Consequences

1. The projected probability of divorce is taken from U.S. National Center for Health Statistics, Vital and Health Statistics, series 3, no. 19, "National Estimates of Marital Dissolution and Survivorship" (Washington, U.S. Government Printing Office, 1980). The projected proportion of women single at age thirty is from Maurice J. Moore and Carolyn Rogers, "Some New Measurements of First Marriage, 1954 to 1977," paper presented at the annual meeting of the Population Association of America, Philadelphia, April 28, 1979. The projected proportion ever remarrying is discussed below and is described in detail in Appendix 4.

2. For more detail on the sources of data discussed in this section, see Appendix 4.

3. See Appendix 4.

4. U.S. Bureau of the Census, Current Population Reports, series P-23, no. 107, "Families Maintained by Female Householders" (Washington: U.S. Government Printing Office, 1980).

5. U.S. Bureau of the Census, Current Population Reports, series P-20, no. 297, "Number, Timing, and Duration of Marriages and Divorces in the United States: June 1975" (Washington: U.S. Government Printing Office, 1976).

6. James A. Sweet, "The Living Arrangements of Separated, Widowed, and Divorced Mothers," Demography 9 (Feb. 1972): 143–157; George Masnick and Mary Jo Bane, The Nation's Families: 1960–1990 (Cambridge, Mass.: Joint Center for Urban Studies of MIT and Harvard University, 1980); and Ethel Shanas, "Older People and Their Families: The New Pioneers," Journal of Marriage and the Family 42 (Feb. 1980): 9–15.

7. Masnick and Bane, The Nation's Families.

8. Mary Jo Bane, Here to Stay: American Families in the Twentieth Century (New York: Basic Books, 1976).

9. For now-classic statements on the "loss of functions" and the specialization of the family in emotional support and child socialization, see William F. Ogburn, "The Changing Family," The Family 19 (1938): 139–143; and Talcott Parsons and Robert F. Bales, Family, Socialization, and Interaction Process (New York: Free Press, 1955).

10. Judith Blake, "Structural Differentiation and the Family: A Quiet Revolution," in Amos H. Hawley, ed., Societal Growth: Processes and Implications (New York: Free Press, 1979), pp. 179–201.

11. See, for example, E. Mavis Hetherington, Martha Cox, and Roger Cox, "Family Interaction and the Social, Emotional, and Cognitive Development of Children Following Divorce," in V. Vaughn and T. B. Brazelton, eds., The Family: Setting Priorities (New York: Science and Medicine Publishing Co., 1979).

12. Robert S. Weiss, Marital Separation (New York: Basic Books, 1975).

13. E. Mavis Hetherington, Martha Cox, and Roger Cox, "The Aftermath of Divorce," in J. H. Stevens, Jr., and M. Matthews, eds., Mother-Child, Father-Child Relations (Washington: National Association for the Education of Young Children, 1978), pp. 146–176.

14. Weiss, Marital Separation.

15. Judith S. Wallerstein and Joan Berlin Kelly, Surviving the Breakup: How Children and Parents Cope with Divorce (New York: Basic Books, 1980).

16. E. Mavis Hetherington, "Children and Divorce," in R. Henderson, ed., Parent-Child Interaction: Theory, Research, and Prospect (New York: Academic Press, 1980).

17. Hetherington, Cox, and Cox, "Aftermath of Divorce."

18. Wallerstein and Kelly, Surviving the Breakup.

19. Nicholas Zill, "Divorce, Marital Happiness and the Mental Health of Children: Findings from the FCD National Survey of Children," paper presented at the NIMH Workshop on Divorce and Children, Bethesda, Maryland, Feb. 7–8, 1978.

20. Wallerstein and Kelly, Surviving the Breakup.

21. Robert S. Weiss, Going It Alone: The Family Life and Social Situation of the Single Parent (New York: Basic Books, 1979).

22. Elizabeth Herzog and Cecilia E. Sudia, "Children in Fatherless Fami-

lies," in B. M. Caldwell and N. H. Riccuiti, eds., *Review of Child Development Research*, vol. 3 (Chicago: University of Chicago Press, 1973), pp. 141–232.

23. Thomas J. Espenshade, "The Economic Consequences of Divorce," *Journal of Marriage and the Family* 41 (Aug. 1979): 615–625, at p. 623.

24. U.S. Bureau of the Census, Current Population Reports, series P-23, no. 106, "Child Support and Alimony: 1978" (Washington: U.S. Government Printing Office, 1980); Saul Hoffman, "Marital Instability and the Economic Status of Women," *Demography* 14 (Feb. 1977): 67–76; and Carol Adaire Jones, Nancy M. Gordon, and Isabel V. Sawhill, "Child Support Payments in the United States," Working Paper no. 992–03 (Washington: Urban Institute, 1976). Cited in Espenshade, "The Economic Consequences of Divorce."

25. Hoffman, "Marital Instability and the Economic Status of Women."

26. Weiss, *Going It Alone.*

27. Janet A. Kohen, Carol A. Brown, and Roslyn Feldberg, "Divorced Mothers: The Costs and Benefits of Female Family Control," in George Levinger and Oliver C. Moles, eds., *Divorce and Separation: Context, Causes, and Consequences* (New York: Basic Books, 1979), pp. 228–245.

28. Mary Jo Bane, "Marital Disruption and the Lives of Children," in Levinger and Moles, *Divorce and Separation,* pp. 276–286.

29. Suzanne H. Woolsey, "Pied Piper Politics and the Child-Care Debate," *Daedalus* 106 (Spring 1977): 127–145.

30. Harriet B. Presser and Wendy Baldwin, "Child Care as a Constraint on Employment: Prevalence, Correlates, and Bearing on the Work and Fertility Nexus," *American Journal of Sociology* 85 (March 1980): 1202–1213.

31. John Demos, *A Little Commonwealth: Family Life in Plymouth Colony* (New York: Oxford University Press, 1970).

32. See Frank F. Furstenberg, Jr., and Graham Spanier, "Marital Dissolution and Generational Ties," paper presented at the annual meeting of the Gerontological Society, San Diego, Nov. 1980.

33. Wallerstein and Kelly, *Surviving the Breakup,* reported that the inclusion of the noncustodial father in the child's view of his family is common when the father continues to see the child.

34. Paul Bohannan, "Divorce Chains, Households of Remarriage, and Multiple Divorces," in Paul Bohannan, ed., *Divorce and After* (New York: Doubleday, 1970), pp. 127–139.

35. See my article, "Remarriage as an Incomplete Institution," *American Journal of Sociology* 84 (Nov. 1978): 634–650, from which I draw heavily in this section.

36. On the legal ambiguities concerning remarriages, see Lenore J. Weitzman, "Legal Regulation of Marriage: Tradition and Change," *California Law Review* 62 (1974): 1169–1288.

37. Bohannan, "Divorce Chains."

38. I. Fast and A. C. Cain, "The Stepparent Role: Potential for Disturbances in Family Functioning," *American Journal of Orthopsychiatry* 36 (April 1966): 485–491.

39. For a review, see Cynthia Longfellow, "Divorce in Context: Its Impact on Children," in Levinger and Moles, *Divorce and Separation,* pp. 287–306.

40. Zill, "Divorce, Marital Happiness, and the Mental Health of Children."

41. Neil Kalter, "Children of Divorce in an Outpatient Psychiatric Population," *American Journal of Orthopsychiatry* 47 (Jan. 1977): 40–51.

42. Kalter, "Children of Divorce," argues similarly. On the lack of incest taboos in remarriages, see Margaret Mead, "Anomolies in American Postdivorce Relationships," in Bohannan, *Divorce and After,* pp. 107–125.

43. See, for example, Terence C. Halliday, "Remarriage: The More Compleat Institution?" *American Journal of Sociology* 86 (Nov. 1980): 630–635.

44. See Cherlin, *"Remarriage as an Incomplete Institution."*

45. Hetherington, Cox, and Cox, "Aftermath of Divorce"; and William J. Goode, *Women in Divorce* (New York, Free Press, 1956).

46. Wallerstein and Kelly, *Surviving the Breakup.*

47. See, for example, Hallowell Pope and Charles W. Mueller, "The Intergenerational Transmission of Marital Instability," in Levinger and Moles, *Divorce and Separation,* pp. 99–113.

48. Glen H. Elder, Jr., *Children of the Great Depression* (Chicago, University of Chicago Press, 1974).

49. Weiss, *Going It Alone.*

50. See, for example, Goode, *Women in Divorce.*

51. U.S. National Center for Health Statistics, Monthly Vital Statistics Report, vol. 28, no. 12, "Births, Marriages, Divorces and Deaths for 1979" (Washington, U.S. Government Printing Office, 1980).

4. Black-White Differences

1. Ronald R. Rindfuss and James A. Sweet, *Postwar Fertility Trends and Differentials in the United States* (New York: Academic Press, 1977).

2. Elise F. Jones and Charles F. Westoff, "The End of 'Catholic' Fertility," *Demography* 16 (May 1979): 209–217; and James McCarthy, "Religious Commitment, Affiliation, and Marital Dissolution," in Robert Wuthnow, ed., *The Religious Dimension* (New York: Academic Press, 1979), pp. 179–197.

3. On fertility trends by race, see Rindfuss and Sweet, *Postwar Fertility Trends.* On divorce, see Paul Jacobson, *American Marriage and Divorce* (New York: Rinehart, 1959); and U.S. National Center for Health Statistics, Vital and Health Statistics, series 21, no. 22, "Divorces: Analysis of Changes, United States, 1969" (Washington: U.S. Government Printing Office, 1973).

4. Until the 1960s, most national statistics were tabulated only by "color" (white versus nonwhite), not by "race" (white versus black). But the vast majority—usually 90 percent or more—of people in the nonwhite category were black.

5. Most young black women eventually will marry, out the minority that may never do so is growing. In 1979, 13 percent of all black women aged thirty-five to forty-four had never married (compared to 6 percent for whites), and this percentage may increase in the 1980s as the many younger black women who are currently remaining single grow older. For 1979 data, see U.S. Bureau of the Census, Current Population Reports, series P-20, no. 349, "Marital Status and Living Arrangements: March 1979" (Washington: U.S. Government Printing Office, 1980).

6. On the trends since 1940 see U.S. National Center for Health Statistics, Vital and Health Statistics, series 21, no. 36, "Trends and Differentials in Births to Unmarried Women: United States, 1970–76" (Washington: U.S.

Government Printing Office, 1980). On out-of-wedlock childbearing rates, see U.S. National Center for Health Statistics, Vital Statistics Report, Advance Report, vol. 29, no. 1, supplement, "Final Natality Statistics, 1978" (Washington: U.S. Government Printing Office, 1980).

7. Andrew Cherlin, "Postponing Marriage: The Influence of Young Women's Work Expectations," *Journal of Marriage and the Family* 42 (May 1980): 355–365.

8. Surveys of adolescents conducted in 1971, 1976, and 1979 by Melvin Zelnik and John F. Kantner showed that unmarried, pregnant adolescents were increasingly likely to terminate their pregnancies by abortion. Moreover, the proportion of unmarried adolescents who married before they resolved their pregnancies (though birth, miscarriage, or abortion) declined. See Melvin Zelnik and John F. Kantner, "Sexual Activity, Contraceptive Use and Pregnancy among Metropolitan-Area Teenagers: 1971–1979," *Family Planning Perspectives* 12 (Sept./Oct. 1980): 230–237.

9. Cherlin, "Postponing Marriage."

10. Center for Health Statistics, "Trends and Differentials in Births to Unmarried Women."

11. These differences in marital disruption appear to hold, even controlling for differences between blacks and whites in educational attainment and in age at marriage. See W. Parker Frisbie, Frank D. Bean, and Isaac W. Eberstein, "Patterns of Marital Instability among Mexican Americans, Blacks, and Anglos," in Frank D. Bean and W. Parker Frisbie, eds., *The Demography of Racial and Ethnic Groups* (New York: Academic Press, 1978), pp. 143–163.

12. The data used in constructing Figure 4-3 and calculating the index values in Table 4-1 were not standardized for changes in age composition. Further calculations showed that in this narrow age range—twenty-five to forty-four—shifts in age composition had a negligible effect on the changing distribution of marital status by color (or race) by sex.

13. Chicago: University of Chicago Press, 1939.

14. Daniel P. Moynihan, "The Negro Family: The Case for National Action," in Lee Rainwater and William L. Yancey, *The Moynihan Report and the Politics of Controversy* (Cambridge, Mass.: MIT Press, 1967), pp. 41–124.

15. Herbert G. Gutman, *The Black Family in Slavery and Freedom, 1750–1925* (New York: Pantheon, 1976), pp. 455–456. For a review of this and similar studies, see Stanley L. Engerman, "Black Fertility and Family Structure in the U.S., 1880–1940," *Journal of Family History* 2 (Summer 1977): 117–138.

16. Gutman, *Black Family in Slavery and Freedom.*

17. Current Population Reports, series P-20, no. 349.

18. Frank F. Furstenberg, Jr., Theodore Hershberg, and John Modell, "The Origins of the Female-Headed Black Family: The Impact of the Urban Experience," *Journal of Interdisciplinary History* 6 (Autumn 1975): 211–233.

19. Gutman, *Black Family in Slavery and Freedom.*

20. Larry H. Long and Kristen A. Hansen, "Trends in Return Migration to the South," *Demography* 12 (Nov. 1975): 601–614.

21. U.S. Bureau of the Census, Current Population Reports, series P-23, no. 42, "The Social and Economic Status of the Black Population in the United States, 1971" (Washington: U.S. Government Printing Office, 1972); and Current Population Reports, series P-23, no. 107, "Families Maintained by Female Householders" (Washington, U.S. Government Printing Office, 1980).

Women who are maintaining families, according to the Census Bureau's definition, include widowed and single women who head families, women whose husbands are in the armed forces or otherwise away from home involuntarily, as well as women who are heading families and who are separated from their husbands through divorce or marital discord. Women who are married with their husbands present are excluded. For a review of nineteenth-century studies, see Engerman, "Black Fertility and Family Structure."

22. William Julius Wilson, "The Declining Significance of Race," *Society*, (Jan./Feb. 1978): 56; see also William Julius Wilson, *The Declining Significance of Race* (Chicago: University of Chicago Press, 1978).

23. As early as 1960 there were some indications that the pattern of change in marital status for better-educated blacks differed from the pattern for those with less education. Reynolds Farley, a demographer who has studied the black population extensively, examined decennial census data from 1940 to 1960 and tentatively suggested that "among Negroes who have experienced socio-economic gains, marital stability is increasing while among those who have not experienced such gains, marital instability is continuing to increase." See Reynolds Farley, *Growth of the Black Population* (Chicago: Markham, 1970), p. 159.

24. Carol B. Stack, *All Our Kin* (New York: Harper and Row, 1974).

25. Engerman, "Black Fertility and Family Structure."

26. U.S. President, *Employment and Training Report of the President, 1980* (Washington: U.S. Government Printing Office, 1980).

27. See Suzanne M. Bianchi and Reynolds Farley, "Racial Differences in Family Living Arrangements and Economic Well-Being: An Analysis of Recent Trends," *Journal of Marriage and the Family* 41 (Aug. 1979): 537–551. Some observers believe that trends in unemployment rates do not adequately reflect the severity of the economic hardships many blacks face. They suggest that the cumulative effect of several postwar recessions—in which some blacks are "last-hired, first-fired"—has been to prevent them from consolidating economic gains made in prosperous years. See Robert B. Hill, "Black Families in the 1970s," in James D. Williams, ed., *The State of Black America 1980* (Washington: National Urban League, 1980), pp. 29–58.

28. See, for example, Heather L. Ross and Isabel V. Sawhill, *Time of Transition: The Growth of Families Headed by Women* (Washington: Urban Institute, 1975).

29. Daphne Spain and Larry H. Long, "Black Movers to the Suburbs: How Many are Moving to White Neighborhoods" U.S. Bureau of the Census, Center for Demographic Studies, forthcoming.

30. See, for example, Michael Novak, "Race and Truth," *Commentary* 62 (Dec. 1976): 54–58.

31. For reviews of this evidence, see Oliver C. Moles, "Public Welfare Payments and Marital Dissolution: A Review of Recent Studies," in George Levinger and Oliver C. Moles, eds., *Divorce and Separation: Context, Causes, and Consequences* (New York: Basic Books, 1979), pp. 167–180; and Stephen J. Bahr, "The Effects of Welfare on Marital Stability and Remarriage," *Journal of Marriage and the Family* 41 (Aug. 1979): 533–560. Some studies suggest that the effect of welfare benefits may act through decreasing the likelihood that a single parent will remarry more than through increasing the likelihood of marital dissolution; see Bahr, "Effects of Welfare," and Ross and Sawhill, *Time*

of Transition. Another recent report suggests that instituting a guaranteed minimum income program might increase the likelihood of marital dissolution among the low-income population; see Michael T. Hannan, Nancy Brandon Tuma, and Lyle P. Groeneveld, "Income and Marital Events: Evidence from an Income Maintenance Experiment," *American Journal of Sociology* 82 (May 1977): 1186–1211.

32. See Stack, *All Our Kin;* Andrew Billingsley, *Black Families in White America* (Englewood Cliffs, N.J.: Prentice-Hall, 1969); and Robert Hill, *The Strengths of Black Families* (New York: Emerson-Hall, 1972).

33. Stack, *All Our Kin.*

34. Bianchi and Farley, "Racial Differences in Family Living Arrangements."

Index